MW01124194

The Compatibility Matrix

The Qualities of
YOUR Ideal Mate

HEATHER COLLINS GRATTAN

Copyright © 2011 Heather Collins Grattan
All rights reserved.
ISBN-10: 146351249X
ISBN-13: 978-1463512491

DEDICATION

In loving memory of
Nugget I, Nugget II, Pepper, Muffy, Snowball, and Jake—
our canine bundles of unconditional love—
who are now playing a Heavenly game of fetch with
Holly Solomon, Matt Jordan, Brian Montes,
and a host of other loved ones.
Our loss is Heaven's gain.

Table of Contents

Foreword
by Joseph "Dr. Joe" Christiano

As one who believes that true compatibility among couples is more than merely holding hands or sharing lunch together, Heather Collins Grattan has done a marvelous job integrating a multidimensional approach in *The Compatibility Matrix*.

It is said of couples who hit it off really well that they had "good chemistry." Heather touches upon that topic with insights that will open your thought process when searching for Mr. or Ms. Right. With her research on the link between personality traits and one's chemistry, *The Compatibility Matrix* becomes a personal road map for discovering that most compatible mate.

In my profession, I have found it extremely interesting how our genetic individuality—including the outcome of our health and fitness condition—is directly correlated with food and one's blood type. The outcome of maximizing results for one's illness profile, ideal weight, and the overall sense of well-being is always profoundly optimal due to this correlation.

From a purely personal perspective, and seeing how *The Compatibility Matrix* provides multiple considerations when searching for that "right" partner, I see strong parallels with my own married life.

Having gone through one marriage, the prospects of another seemed rather unlikely. Maybe controlled by fear, emotional pain, or just from having had an experience that wasn't exactly what anyone considering the married life should be like, I was fine being single. This negative mindset about seeking a future mate, however, was quickly challenged after meeting Lori.

This time, if there was a "this time," things would be different. This time I was wiser, less motivated to race to the altar, and open to see both similarities and differences—or, better put, compatibility. This time I needed to look at the whole picture.

It is amazing how the compatibility issues played a huge role in the outcome of our relationship. Some of the points found in *The Compatibility Matrix* were the same points of interest that we considered. Lori was Italian, and that was a key point. She wasn't in a hurry to get married, and neither was I. In fact, when we met, we became friends—not lovers. Our faiths were not the same—that changed when Lori accepted Christ as her Savior. She was 14 years younger than me, but she was more mature and I less so, so that gelled well. There were many areas to examine before the big day!

The compatibility list was falling into place. If I'd had a score for our compatibility (like in this book), our scores would have been in our favor…but I still had reservations about taking that big step, even after 5 years of dating her. I needed to be set free myself from the fear of being hurt again before I would be able to feel free in my marriage.

To be free in my marriage I had to make myself vulnerable to Lori. I had to take down the walls I had built up from past experiences. I had to be willing to get hurt but depend and trust her love that she had for me to be free. I found that by taking the time to examine as many aspects of each other as possible, including the pluses and minuses, and to be open to change, that our probability of enjoying a successful partnership and marriage was likely.

After 15 years of marriage plus 6 ½ previous years of dating, we have learned to develop and preserve our compatibility for each other.

The Compatibility Matrix is certainly a book long overdue. I know I could have benefited from it immensely had it come out 21 years ago. This is a must-read book for any concerned individual, whether already in a relationship or searching for a future relationship.

Joseph Christiano, ND, CNC

Preface

> *"The good news about marriage in America is that divorce is going down; so Americans who are getting married seem to be making wiser choices. The bad news is that fewer and fewer Americans are getting married in the first place, and are often cycling through a number of partners in ways that are destructive for themselves and any children that they have."*
>
> **– Bradford Wilcox, NMP**
> **Director, The National Marriage Project, University of Virginia**
> **www.virginia.edu/MarriageProject**

I've often observed couples and wondered: What made them choose *each other* over the hundreds or thousands of others they've met? It has to be more than the usual suspects: looks and personality. It can't even be just your Uncle George's theory of "The secret to a happy marriage is two bathrooms!" or your Aunt Sally's theory of "The secret to a happy marriage is a sense of humor."

It's deeper than that. It's perspective. It's Chemistry. It's having an eerily similar outlook, things you enjoy doing, and things you value. (After all, *your* idea of a sense of humor is different from your Aunt Sally's idea of a sense of humor. And if you start out in marriage with only one bathroom, that can't be a dealbreaker.)

Sure, you need a *good* person, someone who treats you well—so what do you look for beyond the obvious? Every person comprises a complex set of characteristics, including "baggage," and it's a matter of finding someone who is closely compatible with your own set of characteristics—in addition to being someone you're actually attracted to.

I'm functioning as a reporter in this book, albeit with a somewhat home-spun approach. Although this is based on research, it's the sort of research that really can't have "double-blind, placebo-controlled" results that would satisfy a scientist, because compatibility is both art and science—so you'll notice that each factor in this book offers a balance of strictness and flexibility, to help you analyze the people you're dating in regards to how compatible they're likely to be with you on a long-term basis. Because if you fall in love with a person and get married, you'll want to stay "in like" with that person so you don't feel stuck. This survey has helped flesh out the things that make people stay "in like" and keep enjoying each other.

I've been happily married since age 22, and in retrospect I feel so fortunate that I had had such excellent parental guidance as to what I should personally look for in a spouse—i.e., look for someone with whom I share a lot in common. "Don't marry someone because you feel sorry for him!" was one of my Dad's mantras. (He's a Presbyterian minister and has counseled many couples over the years, and apparently he saw the "feeling sorry for" phenomenon in more marriages than you'd think.)

And in the spirit of my Dad's mantra, I knew I should feel attracted to the man I married: Marriage shouldn't be a "project" to change the other person for the better, in your judgment. Even if that worked (and it usually doesn't), the gratification of doing so quickly seeps away when little arguments crop up about the dishes or toilet paper.

Many of the most heated disputes that caused couples to visit my Dad for counseling involved money—disagreements over finances—so I knew I would fit best with a guy who had a similar socioeconomic background as I did. I also knew that I'd get along best with someone who had similar religious and political views as I did, because everyone knows that the two hot-button issues to avoid in polite conversation are Religion and Politics; I didn't want to have to avoid discussing something that comes to the forefront as often as every Sunday or every election.

And then I read the fascinating finding about blood-type tendencies in couples. Joseph Christiano and Steven M. Weissberg happened to notice a trend among their married participants during their study of exercise consistencies among people of the various blood types.[1] And I realized that this finding was consistent in my own marriage and in other happy marriages around me. Hmmm.

The Evolution of the Compatibility Matrix and the RESPECT Principle

After considering all these pieces of the compatibility puzzle, I decided to try to solve it by determining whether the pieces *consistently* fit together the way they indeed fit in the happy marriages within my own realm. I created a one-page survey, asked my Mom to edit it (she deleted some questions and added others, based on her own knowledge thanks to her psychology degree), and handed it out it to more than 500 couples— giving them a self-addressed stamped envelope in which to send it back, so they could be completely anonymous if they wanted. More than 250 couples sent theirs back to me, and this information provided the empirical data which shaped this book. Each couple's survey had three columns: The questions, His answers, and Her answers. The "His" and "Hers" answers formed each couple's Compatibility Matrix.

Some of the questions on this survey received very consistent answers among the couples, and it's these principles that we'll emphasize in this book. The *inconsistent* factors, where patterns didn't appear to exist, seem to prove to be general *nonissues* in a marriage, because a trend is not demonstrated. These are listed in Chapter 11: Lesser Issues in Compatibility. (Hint: Age and race are two nonissues.)

All of the consistent factors were organized into the neat acronym RESPECT: Religion, Education, Spending, Politics, Environment (a two-parter), Chemistry, and Togetherness. Read on to see how it all crystallized and how it applies to you.

Note: Because the English language is devoid of a gender-neutral singular personal pronoun, I will use "they" and "their" throughout this book to avoid the awkward "s/he" or "he or she." Capitalizations are also used throughout to help aid readability, so that terminologies specific to this book don't blur with adjacent text.

Chapter 1: Why This Book Is Different

Aren't you tired of magazines, books, Web sites, and experts telling you the one thing you really need in an ideal mate? Some brilliant psychologists and counselors have even devised complicated compatibility methods that are just too unwieldy or vague to be applied in real life: One Web site lists 29 areas in which you should match with someone (and you'd better hope Mr/s. Right happens to be signed up there as well!); another book lists tons of quizzes; yet another book lists three huge areas that require a lot of insightfulness, introspection, and self-analysis. (Are you up to the task?)

Many people have indeed found Mr/s. Right on matchmaking Web sites, but that doesn't help if you just want to know whether the person you're dating might truly be a good match for you in marriage.

There's got to be an easier way, and there is: The simple Compatibility Matrix grid is just a few basic, cut-and-dry factors about a person. Your Matrix will clearly show how closely you match with someone else, because half of the Matrix is about you, and the other half is about the other person. There's even a Cheat Sheet later in the book.

After all, you don't need only "one thing" in a spouse, and 29 might seem a bit impossible, but seven—which is the goal here—is doable. You need the basics, and you should be strict with yourself not to settle for less than you want.

The Compatibility Matrix uses the RESPECT Principle to help define your own individual basics and to define what precisely to look for— the sort of traits that are the best match for you. RESPECT is an acronym.

How the Compatibility Matrix Solves the Puzzle

In analyzing the results of the Matrix survey (which is explained in the latter half of the Preface), the respondents had an average score of 7, with the happiest marriages (judging by observation to the best of my ability) scoring 7 or 8, and the somewhat-less-happy marriages generally scoring below that. So I narrowed it down to eight basic areas necessary for lifelong compatibility, with a "Perfect" score of 7 and an "Ideal" score of 8.

Given a possible score of 8 but a goal of 7, a slight mismatch in one of the eight areas doesn't necessarily have to be that big of a deal. I even had to include Professional Extra Credit for cases in which you and Mr/s. Right are both in the same field or profession, so you actually might end up with a Perfect score of 7 even if you mismatch on one or two—this is because I noticed that several perfectly happy marriages in the survey scored only a 6, but upon further reflection I noticed that they share the same professional areas as their spouses. (That said, their mismatched areas were not in the more hot-button areas like Religion.)

That said, don't rationalize big-time mismatched areas just because you're very attracted to the other person or are in the same general profession. If you're dating someone and you really like them, give it plenty of time, go out on plenty of dates together, and pay attention to how things prove out. Don't avoid discussing difficult subjects—that's a big part of the dating process. If you wait until you're married to have the in-depth talks about your values and beliefs, it will be too late. This book's purpose is to help you not only to find someone to marry, and not only to avoid divorce, but to find a person with whom you can have a fun and fulfilling marriage!

And let's get one thing out in the open right away: The mantra of "opposites attract" is true, but the fact that you're man and woman is opposite enough. In fact, it's just right. God made it perfectly so. Too much more oppositeness will bring full-blown opposition, so keep in mind that you're looking for someone who's a lot like you.

Remember: There Is Only One *You*

Happy marriages have certain basic things in common. First of all, couples *have things in common!* One bride-to-be told my Dad that the reason her first marriage failed was because they "didn't have enough similarities." (Her groom-to-be was a much better fit, she said.) Indeed, the differences between spouses in a successful marriage are rarely terribly divisive to begin with—and if a major difference does exist, the couple figures out a way to avoid the issue or to compromise. But you can't compromise or reason together as a married couple unless you first share a lot of common ground.

You have a unique combination of qualities, experiences, and values that can be the perfect match for someone else, and the Matrix scale will help you identify those key traits. Keep in mind that one person's Prince/-ss Charming is another person's frog, and you'll kiss a lot of frogs while on your mission. (One friendly note: Avoid doing anything that might produce tadpoles, lest you be forever entangled with a mismatched frog!)

But I don't mean to disparage perfectly good people as "frogs." Henry Garipey said it more eloquently: "Every life is a fresh thought from the mind of God. No two are the same." He's right. There is only one you, and you're a great match for someone.

No matter what you've been through in the past, you can regroup and start fresh. This book admittedly tries to transform an art—the art of matchmaking—into a quasi-science, but you have to start somewhere—and getting down to basics is always a good approach. Even artists begin with the basics: basic colors or pencil upon a plain surface. The search for your ideal mate begins with a clean slate, and this book will help keep you focused.

In the following chapters, we'll explore the trends found among this study's participants, and we'll talk about how you can apply this knowledge in your own life. Enjoy reading the magazine-style vignettes, and notice the patterns.

Chapter 2: The RESPECT Principle and Your Own Matrix

In analyzing the results of the Compatibility Matrix survey, a set of shared characteristics emerged among happy couples of all different nationalities, religions, and races. I was amazed at how consistent certain things were among the married couples I surveyed—and yet, the results are very comfortably natural…and almost painfully obvious! They are:

Religion
Education
Spending
Politics
Environment
Chemistry
Togetherness

…because it all boiled down to *respecting* each other on a very deep level, so much so that you *agree* with each other about many, many things—even the ways you react to things. Happily married couples understand each other in these basic ways.

If a couple thoroughly respects each other in everyday ways, they communicate more naturally, and they can therefore get past any stupid argument that arises from when one or both are hungry or tired. And let's face it, it's little things like this that ultimately keep a marriage running smoothly or, if major discrepancies exist, sputtering along in a relatively joyless marriage.

In other words, if the two of you can get along and understand each other on the small issues that arise on a daily basis, you'll be able to handle the larger issues together as well.

So get excited, because we're about to figure out what kind of person you should be looking for!

Quickly Create Your Own Personal Compatibility Matrix

Before reading any further in this book, please fill out the following ultra-short survey for yourself. You can then refer to it as you read further along. This is your "half" of the Compatibility Matrix, which uses the RESPECT Principle to match up your half (below) with someone else's half. As you date people, you can track how well your Matrix correlates with each of them in the Romance Tracker later in the book. Remember: There are no wrong answers. Enjoy!

	You
R (Religion): What is your religion or religious affiliation?	(Please write your religion on the line below:) _____ Importance (1=Very; 4=Not very): 1 2 3 4
E (Education): What is the highest education level/degree you've completed?	☐ Jr. High School ☐ High School ☐ Some College/Associate's ☐ Bachelor's ☐ Master's ☐ Doctorate
S (Spending): How frugal are you?	1=Very; 4=Not very: 1 2 3 4
P (Politics): What is your political bent?	1=Conservative; 4=Liberal: 1 2 3 4
E (Environment part 1): What is your birth order (i.e., your role in the family environment while growing up)?	☐ Only-Child ☐ Firstborn of ___ (how many?) ☐ Middle child, number ___ of ___ (how many?); my next-oldest sibling was ___ years older than I, and my next-youngest sibling was ___ years younger than I ☐ Lastborn of ___ (how many?); my next-oldest sibling was ___ years older than I
E (Environment part 2): How important to you are neat-and-clean surroundings?	1=Very important; 4=Not very important: 1 2 3 4
C (Chemistry): What is your blood type?	O A B AB
T (Togetherness): What are your favorite activities to do?	

RESPECT

Chapter 3: Religion

What is your religion or religious affiliation?	(Please write your religion on the line below:)
	Importance (1=Very; 4=Not very): 1 2 3 4

"Or what does a believer have in common with an unbeliever?"
— 2 Corinthians 6:15

Why This Is Important

In the survey, an amazing 95.5% of respondents shared the same Religion within their marriages: Christians married Christians (including many Protestant-and-Catholic matchups), Jews married Jews, and so on. On the 1–4 scale of Importance (see the box above), most couples ranked themselves the same as each other in the importance of Religion (1&1, 2&2, etc.) or only one "notch" apart (e.g., 2&3).

Only 14 of the 241 married couples who answered this question ranked themselves as two notches away from each other (1&3 or 2&4), and a scant nine couples were 1&4—on opposite ends of the Religion spectrum.

These statistics illustrate how people are consistently drawn to each other, and stay together, when they have similar religious convictions.

An apropos Bible passage that applies to people of any Religion warns against being "unequally yoked" in marriage, which alludes to two oxen being in a yoke—if one pulls too much in one direction, it puts stress on the other and may even cause pain. Similarly, if two people are too different theologically, you'll be pulling in opposite directions and won't be able to communicate along the same lines in this major issue.

The Goal

Who you're most compatible with: *You should be of the same Religion as Mr/s. Right, and you should be the same number or only one notch apart on the 1–4 scale of Religious importance.*

This factor has a lot of flexibility, though—e.g., Protestants can marry Catholics and have a perfectly happy marriage, because their shared bottom line is Jesus, and their shared Bible includes the Old and New Testaments. Likewise, Conservative or Reform or Orthodox or Hassidic Jews all share the same basic Jewish background and Hebrew Scriptures (which Christians refer to as the Old Testament). All Muslims share a focus on Mohammed's teachings in the Qur'an.

The world's major Religions have fragmented over disagreements or customs throughout history, because our opinions and beliefs matter to us. They matter a lot. Your faith is what you believe in your heart about the Creator and your relationship and role therein.

All you need to be concerned about is your own beliefs—and then you can talk about those beliefs with those you date to find the right match for you. Remember, it's your broader Religion and Religious convictions, and not necessarily your own denomination or affiliation, that are important here. You and Mr/s. Right may have strongly similar Religious beliefs but dissimilar backgrounds/affiliations, and it might turn out to be a technicality—you two might be able to work that out just fine. It's something to talk about with each other, when your bellies are full and neither one of you is tired or cranky!

A Caveat: Don't Try to Be a Hero

Is your Religion important to you? If so, don't date someone too long who doesn't share the same basic beliefs. This may seem obvious, but many spiritually devout people have gone into marriage thinking that their spouse would eventually "see the light"—i.e., switching to *their* Religion. But this isn't the right way to enter into a serious relationship, because it assumes that the other person should be "fixed," or adjusted, to match you.

You need to respect and understand—and, ideally, agree with—each other's personal beliefs, or the marriage will fall apart because *you* consider yourself spiritually enlightened and don't understand why the other person won't listen to your theological reasoning (or vice versa).

When two people are in basic theological agreement in a trusting, happy marriage, they will naturally develop a more "self-less" perspective of life and thus greater insight of the Creator, because the very power of love flourishes there.

In this chapter, we'll explore some of the major Religions of the world and learn about some participants in this study who are in happy marriages.

Christianity

Most of the respondents who identified themselves as Christians were married to other Christians, but they weren't always of the same denomination within a marriage. In such cases, since the underlying belief system is the same, such differences appeared to be very well tolerated and didn't cause marriage-shattering arguments.

In Christianity, the bottom line is that Jesus died on the cross for your sins and resurrected on what we celebrate as Easter Sunday—the faith is that Jesus was and is the Jewish Messiah as prophesied in Scripture. If you are Christian, this is your Religion; the denomination or sect to which you belong is your affiliation, not your Religion. The idea of marrying across demarcation lines within the greater Church shouldn't scare you away from a perfectly compatible union, so keep your mind open to possibilities!

Profile R-1: Bill and Laura (Baptist and Presbyterian)

Even though these two are affiliated with different Protestant denominations—indeed, Bill is a Baptist minister—Laura and Bill have spent almost a decade as missionaries in South America together.

Before they got married, they had a major Religion-related disagreement over the issue of baptism. Baptists (and many other churches) practice immersion, or full-body baptism in water, when a person is old enough to make a thoughtful decision about following Jesus; Presbyterians (and many other churches) practice baptism at any age, including infancy if the child's parents choose to have the baby baptized.

Their experience shows that even people of Protestant denominations can have differences! It also shows these disagreements don't have to be relationship-shattering. Laura and Bill were obviously able to get past this issue, because they share a devout Christian faith and so many other things in common.

They have been married for more than 40 years. Look through their Matrix and see how they match up:

	Bill	Laura	Matrix Points:
Religion (importance: 1–4)	Christian (Baptist)—1	Christian (Presbyterian)—1	♥
Education	Bachelor's degree	Bachelor's degree	♥
Spending (1–4)	2	4	–
Politics (1–4)	2	2	♥
Environment:			
▪ **Birth Order**	Lastborn of three (2 years younger than his next-oldest sibling)	Second of six (1 ½ years younger than her older sibling)	♥
▪ **Clean (1–4)**	2	2	♥
Chemistry	Type O	Type A	–
Togetherness	Watch sports, go for walks, bike rides, read to each other		♥
Professional Extra Credit	Both work for Christian ministries, and they were missionaries together		♥
Matrix Score:			7

You can see the many similarities these two share. Laura's status as a Middle-Child makes her compatible with a Lastborn like Bill. (Spoiler alert: The Environment chapter shows that Middle-Children are highly compatible with anyone except Only-Children and Twins.) The Spending and Chemistry factors could be potential weaknesses, but a glance at their Togetherness activities—combined with the other shared factors—demonstrates that they have uncannily similar values and thus plenty of ways to enjoy and appreciate each other. Plus, as we'll explain in more detail later, they get Professional Extra Credit for both working in ministry, particularly their work as missionaries. Thus, they earn a perfect score of 7.

Shared values are extremely important and cannot be underestimated in compatibility.

Profile R-2: Ken and Sheryle (Lutherans)

This Lutheran couple has been blessed with more than 30 years of marriage together, and they've enjoyed participating in church activities—such as helping with their sons' youth group. Here is their Matrix:

	Ken	Sheryle	Matrix Points:
Religion (importance: 1–4)	Christian— Lutheran (2)	Christian— Lutheran (2)	♥
Education	Some college	Master's degree	—
Spending (1–4)	3	3	♥
Politics (1–4)	1	1	♥
Environment:			
▪ **Birth Order**	Lastborn of six (1 year younger than his next-oldest sibling)	Lastborn of two (5 years younger than her next-oldest sibling)	♥
▪ **Clean (1–4)**	2	2	♥
Chemistry	Type A	Type A	♥
Togetherness	Watersports, cooking, wine tasting, movies, reading		♥
Matrix Score:			7

These two share a penchant for gourmet cooking—so on Saturdays, they like to "go over menus during breakfast," then they go grocery shopping together, and later they cook the evening meal together in a way that would make professional chefs proud. This is an impressive marriage-bonding habit that other food aficionados would do well to copy. Plus, a quick glance at their Matrix further demonstrates their shared backgrounds and values. A toast to Ken and Sheryle!

Profile R-3: Lou and Marie (Catholics)

Thirty-eight years of marriage help prove that this devout Catholic couple made the right decision years ago at the altar, and their Ideal score of 8 belies that. If a Catholic child grows up attending mass every week, that child will grow up to be very self-aware of their Catholicism—and loyal to it—almost in the same way that Jewish folks are keenly aware of their Jewish heritage. In contrast, Protestants feel empowered to choose their church: They may grow up Methodist but later move to a new city (for professional reasons or whatever) and join Baptist church, then move again and join a Presbyterian church, and move again and join an Episcopal church…you get the gist. Each individual church is different even within the denominations, and Protestants grow up with this freedom-of-choice mindset, looking for good preachers and friendly congregations.

That said, Catholics can just as happily marry Protestants, because their shared Religion is Christianity. Belief in Jesus as the Messiah is the core of all Christian factions regardless of nomenclature, so therein lies the commonality.

	Lou	Marie	Matrix Points:
Religion (importance: 1–4)	Christian—Catholic (1)	Christian—Catholic (1)	♥
Education	Some college	Some college	♥
Spending (1–4)	3	3	♥
Politics (1–4)	2	2	♥
Environment:			
▪ Birth Order	Third of three (16 years younger than his next-oldest sibling)	Only-Child	♥
▪ Clean (1–4)	1	1	♥
Chemistry	Type A	Type A	♥
Togetherness	Craft/street fairs, shopping, movies, dinner		♥
Matrix Score:			8

Their Matrix shows that they practically mirror each other! Note how much older Lou's next-oldest sibling is, too: The large age gap renders Lou a Virtual Firstborn, which makes for a great match for Only-Child Marie.

In fact, full disclosure: I married into a Catholic family, and I'm Protestant. One fascinating factoid is that, even though my husband is one of six children, only two of them are still married to their first spouses—and both of them married Protestants. The other four are divorced from fellow Catholics.

So I caution Catholics to consider Catholicism a litmus test when looking for Mr/s. Right, because that person might simply be affiliated with a different segment of Christianity.

Judaism

Jewish people often take their heritage very seriously, partly because they are declared to be God's chosen people in the Bible, and partly because their culture's history is rife with other peoples trying to eradicate them; and they are taught about this history from childhood. With horrible accounts of the Holocaust and other events, Jews are keenly aware of their religious heritage, and they identify with it deeply even if they don't attend synagogue regularly or at all.

Profile R-4: Stuart and Priscilla

These two have been married 10 years, they are very successful professionals at a major U.S. corporation. Here is their Matrix:

	Stuart	Priscilla	Matrix Points:
Religion (importance: 1–4)	Jewish (2)	Jewish (2)	♥
Education	Master's degree	Master's degree	♥
Spending (1–4)	1	3	–
Politics (1–4)	3	3	♥
Environment:			
▪ **Birth Order**	Only-Child	Second of two (6 years younger than her older sibling)	♥
▪ **Clean (1–4)**	2	1	♥
Chemistry	Type AB	Type AB	♥
Togetherness	Golf, travel, going out to eat		♥
Professional Extra Credit	Both are business leaders at a major U.S. corporation		♥
Matrix Score:			8

On paper, you can already see why this union is successful: They have a *lot* in common. They have an Ideal score of 8.

First of all, both are Jewish and consider it important. The differing Birth Order is negated by the fact that Priscilla is more than 5 years younger than her older sibling—which renders her as a "Virtual Firstborn," because 5 years amounts to a huge difference in your relationship with a sibling and your perspectives of your role at any given age when you're growing up.

(This concept is explained further in the Environment chapter.) They differ in Spending but are not on completely opposite ends of the spectrum.

Priscilla and Stuart also have strong Chemistry: They both have the rare AB blood type, which describes only about 4% of the U.S. population. The fact that they enjoy going out to eat regularly is a healthy sign, because that is a low-maintenance habit that can be done frequently, and provides a relaxing atmosphere for bonding together. This activity is wonderful in keeping the romance alive in a marriage, because the two of you can just sit and talk, or say nothing at all, and just enjoy each other's company and the atmosphere and the food. Also note that Priscilla and Stuart both enjoy golf. Thus, they share values, have similar backgrounds, and enjoy the same activities.

Profile R-5: Brian and Ann

Brian is the only Jewish participant in this study who ranked Religion as a 1 in importance; this demonstrates that it was extremely important that he marry a Jewish woman. And since Jewish people only comprise about 2% of the total U.S. population, his work was cut out for him. But he did find Ann, and she ranks Religion as being important as well:

	Brian	Ann	Matrix Points:
Religion (importance: 1–4)	Jewish (1)	Jewish (2)	♥
Education	Bachelor's degree	Master's degree	♥
Spending (1–4)	2	4	–
Politics (1–4)	3	3	♥
Environment:			
▪ Birth Order	Lastborn of three (7 years younger than his next-oldest sibling)	Firstborn of two	♥
▪ Clean (1–4)	2	1	♥
Chemistry	Type B	Type A	♥
Togetherness	Dinner together, conversations, vacations		♥
Matrix Score:			7

Note how Ann and Brian share other similarities across the board: They both have college degrees, both are moderately liberal, both are relatively fastidious, and they enjoy talking and having dinner together. And

like Priscilla (in Profile R-4), Brian is rendered as a Virtual Firs,
having a substantial number of years between him and his next-
sibling—so he thereby shares some similar perspectives as Ann, ﹀
true Firstborn. They do differ in the Spending category, but at lea﹩
not on polar opposite ends of the spectrum.

Also, as we'll discuss in greater detail in the Chemistry chap﹅ ﹍,
even though blood Types A and B aren't generally compatible, one thing I
discovered from this survey is that this combination can indeed be
compatible if their Religion is ranked highly and strongly matched between
the two. So the Chemistry factor in Ann and Brian's marriage is just fine.

This is an excellent example of how compatibility is truly an art, in
correlation to the quasi-scientific aspects presented in this book. If you find
someone who "has all the checkmarks," getting a Perfect or Ideal score
when matched up with you, that doesn't necessarily mean they're Mr/s.
Right. Someone else might be better for you who is missing a checkmark or
two, and you two might be able to work around that quirk! That said, **it's
better for the quirk to be in the area of Chemistry or Environment
than in the area of Religion.** If an area is particularly important to you,
make it a necessity (not something that can differ between you and your
mate), and make sure you don't deviate from that standard. You need
someone who reflects and complements *you*.

Islam

As with Christianity and Judaism, Islam isn't the same across the
board—there are different groups within the Religion.

The prophet Mohammed, who is the central figure in Islam,
dictated the Qur'an. Able-bodied Muslims are to try to visit Mohammed's
birthplace city of Mecca at least once during their lives, and this pilgrimage
is called the Hajj. During the month of Ramadan, the ninth month of the
Moslem calendar, an observant Muslim fasts from sunrise until sunset every
day. In the Qur'an, Jews and Christians are referred to as "people of the
Book," demonstrating that Mohammed respected the teachings of the
Bible. He even articulated his belief in the virgin birth of Jesus by Mary.

Just like members of other Religions, a Muslim who is dating a
non-Muslim should discuss Religion before the relationship becomes
very serious.

Profile R-6: Nasser and Cindy

Nasser grew up in Lebanon and Sierra-Leone as a Shi'ite Muslim, and he was even injured during the Gulf War by Saddam Hussein's anti-Shi'ite fighters. He later moved to the United States, where he met Cindy. They've been married for more than 20 years, and are even the parents of triplets! Here is their Matrix:

	Nasser	Cindy	Matrix Points:
Religion (importance: 1–4)	Muslim (1)	Muslim (1)	♥
Education	Bachelor's degree	Bachelor's degree	♥
Spending (1–4)	1	3	–
Politics (1–4)	1	1	♥
Environment:			
▪ Birth Order	Firstborn of five	Lastborn of two (5 ½ years younger than her older sibling)	♥
▪ Clean (1–4)	1	1	♥
Chemistry	Type O	Type O	♥
Togetherness	Spending time with their children, going to a nearby amusement park, boating		♥
Matrix Score:			7

In addition to Religion, almost all of their other factors correspond with each other as well. Cindy is a Lastborn, but she is rendered as a Virtual Firstborn since she is more than 5 years younger than her older sibling. Nasser and Cindy have the same Education level, Political bent, Chemistry, and things they enjoy doing together regularly. Cindy notes that she was not a "1" in Cleanliness until after she married Nasser, and then it became more important to her once they began to have a family.

They both went to Florida State University and enjoy rooting for the Seminoles together—and although it's not imperative that both people in a happy marriage root for the same team, it certainly helps on game days!

Other Religions

Participants in this survey were very diverse in their Religious affiliations or lack thereof, representing everything from Hindu to Wiccan to Russian Orthodox to Mormon to atheist. One couple comprises a Hindu husband and an Episcopalian wife; another is a Wiccan wife married to a Catholic husband.

People in less-represented Religions tend to broaden their scope while dating, not always being too strict when it comes to looking for someone of the *exact* same Religion. But if you are indeed a member of an under-represented Religion in the area of the world in which you live, and if you are a devout member of that Religion, you should marry someone who is of that same Religion. Don't let others talk you out of being picky.

Read more about this in the first section of Chapter 13: Why Some Marriages Don't Work Out.

Final Thoughts on Religion…

The profiled couples featured in this chapter, and throughout this book, demonstrate why sharing the same general views on Religion is of utmost importance to a successful marriage. Otherwise, make sure you've discussed this issue thoroughly before you tie the knot.

If you're developing a serious romantic relationship with someone of another faith—even if Religion isn't very important to either of you, and you're content with a _ESPECT on the Matrix scale—talk about your beliefs (don't sugarcoat it), about expectations within the realm of marriage, and about what Religion the children (if any) would be raised in. For example, what holidays will you celebrate? Would you want to baptize your children, give them a bar/bat mitzvah, or send them to religious training of any kind? And even if there are no children, it's best if you discuss everything from Christmas/Easter celebrations to the long-awaited trip to Mecca for the Hajj, or whatever religious traditions are involved between the two of you.

~ Cheat Sheet ~	
RESPECT	**Answer:**
Religion (and 1–4)	…Look for someone of the same or very similar religion as yourself, **AND** for whom importance about Religion is the same or only one "notch" away from you

RESPECT

Chapter 4: Education

What is the highest education level/degree you've completed?	☐ Jr. High School
	☐ High School
	☐ Some College/Associate's
	☐ Bachelor's
	☐ Master's
	☐ Doctorate

"Do not boast so proudly, or let arrogant words come out of your mouth, for the Lord is a God of knowledge..." — 1 Samuel 2:3

Why This Is Important

A person's level of Education completed is an issue most people readily agree with in regards to compatibility. If one person in a relationship is highly educated and the other person doesn't really value extensive schooling, deep-seated conflict can eventually develop no matter how much Chemistry exists.

This category ultimately reflects a combination of a person's value of the pursuit of knowledge and their family's general attitude toward academics. One of the reasons a similar Education level is important is that otherwise, the more highly educated person may feel intellectually superior to the other, or the less-educated person may feel defensive when the other person spews their knowledge.

The Goal

Who you're most compatible with: *If you've...*
...completed Junior High, you're compatible with someone who has completed up to Some College or an Associate's Degree

…completed High School or Some College, you're compatible with someone who has completed up to a Bachelor's Degree

…earned a Bachelor's Degree, you're compatible with someone who has completed at least Some College

…earned a Master's or Doctorate (Ph.D.), you're compatible with someone who has earned at least a Bachelor's Degree

In this arena, you need to avoid a superiority or inferiority complex from ever developing with your spouse. If the Education levels of the two of you are too disparate, this scenario could turn into a nasty argument—and it could become a *recurring* argument. You don't want your partner to accuse you of being a "showoff" just because you enjoy talking about an intellectual subject, or even about the degree itself. And no one should ever feel like a dummy, or at all intellectually inferior, in a partnership as important as marriage.

Junior High

Two-thirds of the participants who listed junior high as their highest-completed Education level were married to people who had taken some college courses (but didn't receive a bachelor's degree); the other one-third were married to people whose Education level was a high school diploma. None were married to people who had a bachelor's or higher.

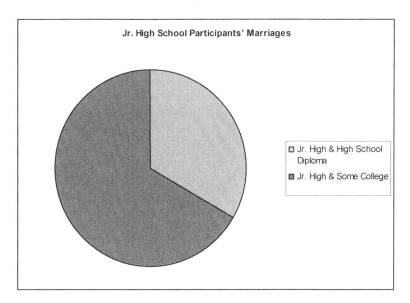

Figure Edu-1: Matrix Study Results of Couples with a Junior High School Spouse

27

Profile Edu-1: Christopher and Ruth

Enjoying almost 60 years together, Ruth and Christopher are a natural fit. On an Educational level, he completed junior high school, and she took some college courses and implemented her skills as an elementary-school aide. Here is their Matrix:

	Christopher	Ruth	Matrix Points:
Religion (importance: 1–4)	Christian—Baptist (1)	Christian—Baptist (1)	♥
Education	Junior high school	Some college	♥
Spending (1–4)	4	2	–
Politics (1–4)	2/3	2/3	♥
Environment:			
▪ **Birth Order**	Firstborn of five	Fifth of 10 (2 years younger than her next-oldest sibling)	♥
▪ **Clean (1–4)**	1	1	♥
Chemistry	Type O	Type O	♥
Togetherness	Traveling, playing cards		♥
Matrix Score:			7

Christopher and Ruth are deeply religious; this couple is also equally fastidious and equally politically moderate, so sparks aren't likely to fly over cleaning up the house or during election season.

They value Education similarly as each other, and they both come from big families. Ruth's family role as a Middle-Child naturally taught her to get along with just about anyone, and it makes her compatible with all other Birth Order types except Only-Children and Twins (as we'll discuss further in the Environment chapter). Ruth's Chris Steakhouse would be so lucky to have been named after this wonderful couple.

High School

The Matrix survey found that folks with a high school diploma and no further schooling are most compatible with people who had completed schooling from a high-school diploma to a bachelor's degree, as you can see in this pie chart:

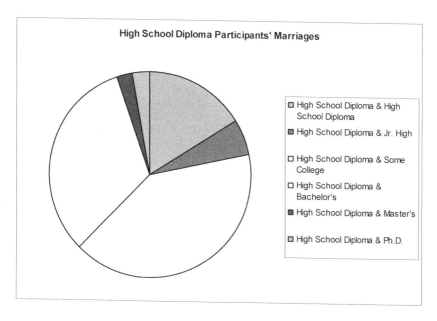

Figure Edu-2: Matrix Study Results of Couples with a High School Diploma Spouse

Profile Edu-2: Kenneth and Dorothy

After each of them lost their spouses to tragic early deaths—his wife to cancer, her husband to an electrical accident—Dorothy and Kenneth "found each other and have had many years of happiness together," she says. "We've been blessed! And life is good!" Their Matrix demonstrates an Ideal score of 8:

	Kenneth	Dorothy	Matrix Points:
Religion (importance: 1–4)	Christian—Presbyterian (1)	Christian—Presbyterian (2)	♥
Education	High school	High school	♥
Spending (1–4)	1	2	♥
Politics (1–4)	2	2	♥
Environment:			
▪ **Birth Order**	Firstborn of five	Only-Child	♥
▪ **Clean (1–4)**	1	2	♥
Chemistry	Type O	Type B	♥
Togetherness	Traveling, golfing, bowling, boating, watersports, visiting with family/friends		♥
Matrix Score:			8

　　　Dorothy and Kenneth both have high school diplomas, and they share similarities in every other area covered in the Matrix. Kenneth's blood type is actually a bit dubious as to its validity (his Reaganesque confidence, charm, and optimism do exude Type O!), but even without that they'd have a Perfect score of 7. They are probably the only participating couple in which they are each other's second marriage while still achieving a full complement of RESPECT values and backgrounds.

Some College

Matrix survey participants who had completed some college (which includes formal post–high school study, including an associate's degree) demonstrated an affinity for those who earned a high-school diploma, some college, or a bachelor's degree.

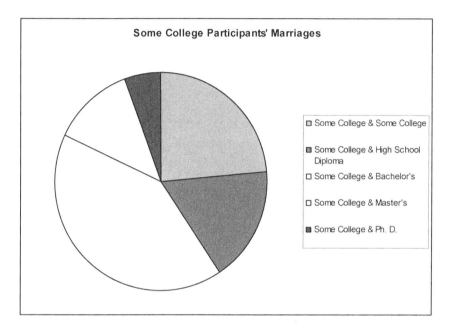

Some College Participants' Marriages

- □ Some College & Some College
- ■ Some College & High School Diploma
- □ Some College & Bachelor's
- □ Some College & Master's
- ■ Some College & Ph. D.

Figure Edu-3: Matrix Study Results of Couples with a Some College Spouse

Profile Edu-3: Jerry and Joyce

Married for more than 50 years, Joyce and Jerry have danced together and stayed active through the years—what a great way to keep the love alive! They both attended some college, and they have a Perfect score of 7 on their Matrix:

	Jerry	Joyce	Matrix Points:
Religion (importance: 1–4)	Christian— Presbyterian	Christian— Presbyterian	♥
Education	Some college	Some college	♥
Spending (1–4)	2	2	♥
Politics (1–4)	2	2	♥
Environment:			
▪ **Birth Order**	Third of seven (2 years younger than his next-oldest sibling)	Only-Child	–
▪ **Clean (1–4)**	1	1	♥
Chemistry	Type A	Type A	♥
Togetherness	Reading, dancing		♥
Matrix Score:			7

Wow—they have the full RESPECT lineup: Religion, Education, Spending, Politics, Environment, Chemistry, and Togetherness. Their only area in which they differ is in the Birth Order component of Environment, as she is an Only-Child whereas he grew up in the middle of a large family. But theirs is a model to be emulated, demonstrating how a Perfect 7 earns them a gold medal in lasting compatibility...a partnership based on deep-seated friendship that blossomed into love.

Bachelor's Degree

Folks with a bachelor's degree proved to be most compatible with people who ranged from having some college to people with doctorates.

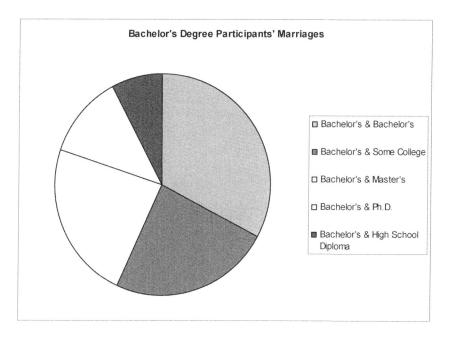

Figure Edu-4: Matrix Study Results of Couples with a Bachelor's Degree Spouse

Profile Edu-4: Bill and Nelle

The most frequently occurring combination of Educational levels among the survey's respondents were couples in which both spouses had earned a bachelor's degree, and Nelle and Bill are a prime example.

After 50 years of marriage, they've proven that two people can come from rival schools—with their respective loyalties—and retain a happy union: Bill went to the University of Florida, Nelle went to Florida State University, and they stay in good humor about their schools' fierce traditional competition. Here is their Matrix:

	Bill	Nelle	Matrix Points:
Religion (im-portance: 1–4)	Christian—Presbyterian (2)	Christian—Presbyterian (2)	♥
Education	Bachelor's degree	Bachelor's degree	♥
Spending (1–4)	2	2	♥
Politics (1–4)	2	2	♥
Environment:			
▪ **Birth Order**	Lastborn of two (3 years younger than his older sibling)	Only-Child	–
▪ **Clean (1–4)**	2	2	♥
Chemistry	Type A	Type AB	♥
Togetherness	Hiking, biking, traveling		♥
Matrix Score:			7

Along with matching perfectly on the Educational level, Nelle and Bill correspond across the board and earn a Perfect score of 7. Their only difference is in Birth Order; however, Bill has only one sibling, and there is a somewhat notable 3-year gap between them. Therefore, this couple shares backgrounds in relatively calm home environments, not with lots of children vying for parental attention.

Profile Edu-5: Bob and LaVerne

Another couple who demonstrate a shared bachelor's degree, LaVerne and Bob, both received their bachelor's degrees and set sail into life. More than 40 years after their nuptials, their Matrix displays why their bond is so strong:

34

	Bob	LaVerne	Matrix Points:
Religion (importance: 1–4)	Christian—Presbyterian (1)	Christian—Presbyterian (1)	♥
Education	Bachelor's degree	Bachelor's degree	♥
Spending (1–4)	2	2	♥
Politics (1–4)	2	3	♥
Environment:			
▪ Birth Order	Lastborn of three (15 years younger than his next-oldest sibling)	Only-Child	♥
▪ Clean (1–4)	3	3	♥
Chemistry	Type A	Type B	♥
Togetherness	Dining out, entertainment/arts events, discussing news events and issues		♥
Matrix Score:			8

Note that both enjoy the arts, treating themselves to evenings at the theater and artistic events. LaVerne loves creating stained-glass windows, so the fact that Bob enjoys the ballet and other artistic pursuits just solidifies their common interests in the arts.

There is a certain intellectual motivation (not necessarily related to Educational level per se, but intellectual nonetheless) in enjoying the theater, symphony, and the like, and this is why enthusiasts deem it an "appreciation." Therefore, such enthusiasts should marry one of their own ilk…or otherwise be relegated to solo trips to the operahouse.

In their Matrix, you can easily see why LaVerne and Bob found each other and stopped looking any further! Although she is an Only-Child whereas he is a Lastborn, he is actually a Virtual Firstborn thanks to the huge 15-year gap between himself and his next-oldest sibling.

And as we'll talk about in the Chemistry chapter, as a Type A and a Type B, their ranking of their shared Religion as a "1" earns them a Chemistry point as well—due to that consistently observed pattern in the Matrix survey. They earn an Ideal score of 8—a work of art indeed.

Master's Degree

Participants with master's degrees proved to be most compatible with people who had earned a bachelor's degree or higher.

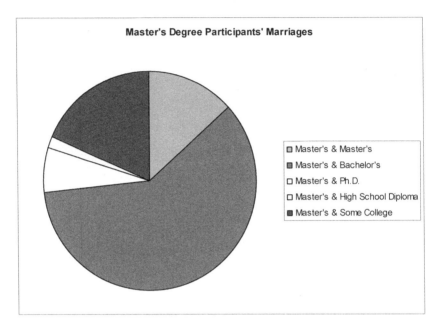

Figure Edu-5: Matrix Study Results of Couples with a Master's Degree Spouse

Profile Edu-6: Ed and Mary Alice

Ed and Mary Alice were married for 33 years before he finally succumbed to the malaria he'd contracted during World War II, but they enjoyed history and intellectual pursuits together during their many years of matrimony. Ed was a professor at Palm Beach State College for many years, and Mary Alice has led historical tours of the Flagler Museum on the island of Palm Beach. Here is their Matrix:

	Ed	Mary Alice	Matrix Points:
Religion (importance: 1–4)	Christian—Presbyterian (2)	Christian—Presbyterian (1)	♥
Education	Master's degree	Master's degree	♥
Spending (1–4)	2	2	♥
Politics (1–4)	2	1	♥
Environment:			
▪ **Birth Order**	Firstborn of two	Firstborn of two	♥
▪ **Clean (1–4)**	4	2	–
Chemistry	Type B	Type O	♥
Togetherness	Historical events		♥
Matrix Score:			7

Mary Alice wrote on her survey that she was initially a "1" regarding Cleanliness, but that it became less important. This is an excellent example of how people tend to adjust to each other's habits and expectations if they really are compatible with each other. And note their many similarities otherwise!

They toured more than 400 U.S. presidential sites of historical significance during their marriage. Mary Alice is also deeply involved in her political party and her church—attending Republican conventions as well as serving as a delegate representing her presbytery at the annual General Assembly of the Presbyterian Church (U.S.A.)—and note that Ed's Political perspective closely matches hers as does his value of Religion. Theirs is an excellent model to follow.

Profile Edu-7: Ludo and Margaret

With a Ideal score of 8 on the Matrix scale, plus more than 45 years of marriage, this multi-degreed couple demonstrate discriminating thoughtfulness for having chosen each other. Ludo is a retired pastor, and he and Margaret live in Canada during the summers and Florida during the winters—pretty nice life! Take a peek at their Matrix:

	Ludo	Margaret	Matrix Points:
Religion (importance: 1–4)	Christian— Presbyterian (1)	Christian— Presbyterian (1)	♥
Education	Doctorate	Master's degree	♥
Spending (1–4)	1	2	♥
Politics (1–4)	3	3	♥
Environment:			
▪ **Birth Order**	Third of four (8 years younger than his next-oldest sibling)	Only-Child	♥
▪ **Clean (1–4)**	1	1	♥
Chemistry	Type A	Type A	♥
Togetherness	Family get-togethers, going to church, traveling, going to the beach, eating out		♥
Matrix Score:			8

She has a master's, and he has a doctorate—demonstrating quite a shared value on higher Education. Note that although Ludo is a Middle-Child, he is rendered a Virtual Firstborn by virtue of the fact that he is a whopping 8 years younger than his next-oldest sibling. Therefore, he's naturally well suited to match up with an Only-Child such as Margaret. And everything else matches perfectly. An Ideal Canadian couple!

Doctorate

Survey participants with a doctorate were most compatible with spouses who had at least a bachelor's degree.

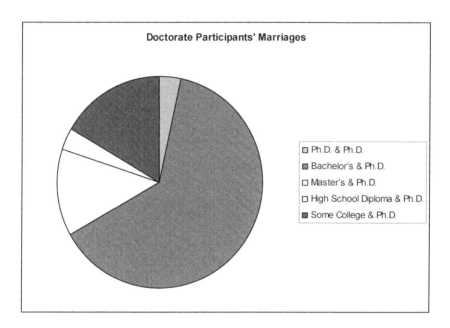

Doctorate Participants' Marriages

- ☐ Ph.D. & Ph.D.
- ■ Bachelor's & Ph.D.
- ☐ Master's & Ph.D.
- ☐ High School Diploma & Ph.D.
- ■ Some College & Ph.D.

Figure Edu-6: Matrix Study Results of Couples with a Doctorate Spouse

Profile Edu-8: Tom and Connie

After more than 20 years together, Connie and Tom keep it together even though she has a busy law practice. Their secret? He stays home and takes care of their two sons. Thus, the modern-day conundrum of two stressed-out professionals who come home to an unsolved set of household issues is simply not that much of a problem here.

Both Tom and Connie are well educated—she with a juris doctorate from law school, and he with a bachelor's degree. They are both devout in their faith, both moderately liberal, and both moderate spenders; also of note is his status as a Virtual Firstborn, since he is more than 5 years younger than his next-oldest sibling—and this matches well with her natural tendencies as the result of being a Firstborn. They match up beautifully, as you can see in their Matrix:

39

	Tom	Connie	Matrix Points:
Religion (importance: 1–4)	Christian— Presbyterian (1)	Christian— Presbyterian (1)	♥
Education	Bachelor's degree	Juris doctorate (law school)	♥
Spending (1–4)	2	3	♥
Politics (1–4)	3	3	♥
Environment:			
▪ Birth Order	Lastborn of three (7 years younger than his next-oldest sibling)	Firstborn of two	♥
▪ Clean (1–4)	3	1	–
Chemistry	Type O	Type O	♥
Togetherness	Tailgating/sports events, eating out, church, children's events		♥
Matrix Score:			7

Final Thoughts on Education...

You can be the smartest, most well-educated person in the world and still not know how to decipher Mr/s. Right (until now). That's because this pursuit isn't only about the intellect, but rather a combination of the mind, body, and soul—which aren't readily evident when you first meet someone, but they can be thoroughly analyzed with the Matrix. (But please don't whip out the Matrix questionnaire for them to answer on the first date! Even though proper analysis requires documentation, keep the checklist at home. It's better to memorize the seven words and bring them up in conversation as naturally as possible.)

Matrix survey results prove that happy couples tend to value Education on the same level as each other, regardless of what the level might be. But beware of a false sense of Chemistry, by interpreting Education and intellectual pursuits as comprising a strong-enough foundation for marriage, e.g., "I just admire him [or her] so much!" Later, in Chapter 13: Why Some Marriages Don't Work Out, you'll meet Angela and her college professor—and you'll hear about why their subsequent marriage didn't last.

~ Cheat Sheet ~	
RESPECT	**Answer: People who completed... Should look for...**
Highest **education** level/degree completed	**Jr. High School...** someone who has earned up to Some College or an Associate's Degree **High School Diploma...** someone who has earned up to a Bachelor's Degree **Some College/Associate's Degree...** someone who has earned up to a Bachelor's Degree **Bachelor's Degree...** someone who has earned at least Some College **Master's Degree...** someone who has earned at least a Bachelor's Degree **Doctorate Degree...** someone who has earned at least a Bachelor's Degree

RESPECT

Chapter 5: Spending

How frugal are you?	1=Very; 4=Not very: 1 2 3 4

> *"...for where your treasure is, there your heart will be also."*
> *— Matthew 6:21*

Why This Is Important

Anyone who has counseled couples will tell you that one of the biggest reasons couples seek marital counseling is due to big disagreements over money. Financial expert and Credit.com co-founder Adam Levin, who was director of the New Jersey State Division of Consumer Affairs, told me that communication about Spending is key to a happy marriage.

"Look for someone who is open about their finances," he says. "It doesn't matter as much if they're a 'spender' or a 'saver,' just as long as you're able to keep up healthy communication about your money-management goals."

Hmm…communication. Brilliantly said. If the two of you are open about your Spending expectations, you'll find out quickly whether you're too dissimilar from each other in this important area.

The Matrix survey found that most successful marriages are made up of people who grew up with similar economic backgrounds. For example, someone who celebrated their 11th birthday with friends at Burger King like I did will not have the same financial perspective as someone whose parents threw a lavish party, or even as someone whose family couldn't afford Burger King without scrimping. Even millionaires who grew up poor still identify with that mentality—so it's a visceral identity we're talking about here—but most people adjust their Spending to their income level. So it's best to talk about things and observe each other's Spending habits.

42

The Goal

Who you're most compatible with: *In Spending, it's best to be the same number or only one "notch" away from the other person on the 1–4 Spending scale.*

Like the Education factor, financial compatibility between two people involves a *lack* of a feeling of superiority or inferiority on both sides. People strongly identify with their socioeconomic situation from a young age, and you may have feelings—possibly subconsciously—of defensiveness toward wealthier people or feelings of socioeconomic dominance over those who aren't as financially advantaged as you. It's all relative.

You have certain financial habits and expectations based on your upbringing, and financial behaviors of others can be observed while dating. If your mother was a waitress, you will expect someone you're dating to treat your waiter with extra respect and dignity, with a friendly smile and a generous tip; but if the person's parents were doctors or lawyers, you might notice a bit of a superiority complex, or unimpressed indifference, toward lower-paid workers. Pay attention to your date's responses and behaviors toward other people.

It's the everyday conduct and attitudes such as these that are important, because they can ultimately cause enormous strife if a strong difference in this area is initially ignored and the relationship continues.

The married couples who participated in this study were asked to rate themselves on a scale of 1 to 4, with 1 being "Very Frugal" and 4 being "Not Very Frugal." A full 45% of the participating couples listed themselves as the same number as each other on the scale (i.e., 1&1, 2&2, 3&3, or 4&4); 38% were only one "notch" apart (1&2, 2&3, or 3&4). Only 13% rated themselves as being two notches apart (1&2 or 2&4), and a tiny 4% of the couples said they're a full three notches apart (1&4), being on completely opposite ends of the Spending spectrum.

Therefore, over 80% of the couples rated themselves as the same number or one notch apart on the Spending scale! Plus, of the 226 couples who answered this question, 57 couples rated themselves as 2&2, and 44 couples rated themselves as 2&3—indicating an overwhelming trend toward general moderation in Spending, and a bit more on the frugal side than not. Only three couples (just 1%) rated themselves as 4&4, and only eight couples (about 4%) said they're 1&1. Interesting stuff—another nod to moderation.

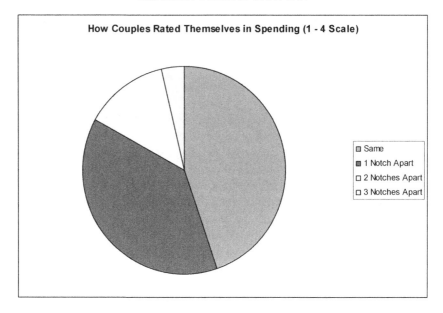

Figure S-1: Overall Matrix Study Results of Spending Tendencies in Marriage

Most people like to spend whimsically every once in a while, and this can be healthy especially if you're investing in *each other*. The telling part is how "every once in awhile" is defined by you personally, and just how the Spending is done: Would you define that as a lavish gift, an expensive dinner out together, or an annual trip across the ocean? Or do you prefer the carpe diem theory, and enjoy a nice dinner out every Friday night even if you don't have much extra cash to spend?

Consider your level of tolerance, too. At what point would you feel like you're Spending too much, or even too little? Buying a pool for the back yard… Taking a trip to an exotic country a couple times a year… Going out to dinner once a week.

People have nuanced, individual layers of tolerance in regards to Spending habits. One participating couple, Bob and Mary Lou, like to scrimp and save for annual trips to Europe. Someone else at their same socioeconomic level may prefer to have a nice dinner out every Friday, year-round, with that same money—they might consider annual trips across the ocean a waste of money because it's so quickly spent. This is an example of how important it is to value Spending money on the same activities, and this is where the Togetherness and the Spending factors coincide.

Very Frugal

Profile S-1: Larry and Ingrid

This highly frugal couple enjoy warm winters in their condo in Florida and mild summers in Connecticut. Some less-frugal people with their income may have bought a large beach house in Florida rather than a condo, but they prefer to be very fiscally conservative. They've been married for more than 50 years, and here is their Matrix:

	Larry	Ingrid	Matrix Points:
Religion (importance: 1–4)	Christian (2)	Christian— Presbyterian (1)	♥
Education	Master's degree	Master's degree	♥
Spending (1–4)	1	1	♥
Politics (1–4)	2	2	♥
Environment:			
▪ Birth Order	Lastborn of three (6 years younger than his next-oldest sibling)	Lastborn of two (4 ½ years younger than her older sibling)	♥
▪ Clean (1–4)	2	2	♥
Chemistry	Type O	Type O	♥
Togetherness	Talking, traveling, reading, sports, walking		♥
Matrix Score:			8

Ingrid and Larry list "talking" and "reading" and "walking" as things they enjoy doing during their free time, and those are very cheap activities! Those pastimes can also be done at the spur of the moment and don't require lots of planning. Simple and low-maintenance are key elements of keeping Spending down to a happy medium.

In addition to considering themselves economically thrifty, notice that they both have master's degrees. Plus, they're both Lastborns who qualify as Virtual Firstborns, so they had similar familial roles while growing up. They have an Ideal score of 8.

Profile S-2: Bob and Joan

In person, Joan and Bob are one of those couples who look like they belong together. They both consider themselves to be very frugal, as well as very fastidious, conservative, and religious. And with an Ideal score of 8, their compatibility proves out on paper as well:

	Bob	Joan	Matrix Points:
Religion (importance: 1–4)	Christian—Presbyterian (1)	Christian—Presbyterian (1)	♥
Education	High school diploma	High school diploma	♥
Spending (1–4)	1	1	♥
Politics (1–4)	2	1	♥
Environment:			
▪ **Birth Order**	Lastborn of three (3 years younger than his next-oldest sibling)	Third of six (2 years younger than her next-oldest sibling)	♥
▪ **Clean (1–4)**	1	1	♥
Chemistry	Type A	Type B	♥
Togetherness	Gardening, bowling, watching TV, babysitting our granddaughter		♥
Matrix Score:			8

Joan's position as a Middle-Child renders her compatible with almost all other Birth Order types, and an added bonus they share is a neat duality as Thirdborns. They also share the same Education levels, and also note their low-maintenance Togetherness activities—easy pastimes that don't require lots of scheduling, if any. As mentioned earlier, couples whose Chemistry comprises A&B who ranked their Religion as 1 or 2 in importance seemed to be highly compatible, so they get a point for Chemistry as well. Their partnership is as Ideal as can be.

Somewhat Frugal

Profile S-3: Marcus and Sandra

Both in editing/writing positions—he, for a Fortune 500 company's Marketing/Advertising department; she, for a large newspaper—Sandra and Marcus not only earn a point for Professional Extra Credit, but they also share a moderately frugal Spending philosophy:

	Marcus	Sandra	Matrix Points:
Religion (importance: 1–4)	Christian (1)	Christian (1)	♥
Education	Bachelor's degree	Bachelor's degree	♥
Spending (1–4)	2	2	♥
Politics (1–4)	2	2	♥
Environment:			
▪ **Birth Order**	Firstborn of two	Lastborn of 13 (1 year younger than her next-oldest sibling)	–
▪ **Clean (1–4)**	1	3	–
Chemistry	Type B	Type O	♥
Togetherness	Watching movies, attending activities with our daughter		♥
Professional Extra Credit	Both are in the field of journalism		♥
Matrix Score:			7

These two aren't likely to argue over financial matters, because they both rated themselves as a moderate 2 on the Spending scale: Fairly frugal, but not overly so. Although they have discrepancies in the two Environment aspects, they match beautifully in all of the other areas. And they earn that Perfect score of 7 thanks to their shared vocational field.

Sandra and Marcus enjoy going to the movies with their daughter every weekend, and they attend their daughter's gymnastics events regularly. They also participate in a host of church activities as a family. They exemplify how well-thought-out routines, including family-bonding activities that involve moderate Spending habits like going to the movies, can make for a fun lifestyle everyone enjoys.

This couple first met at a company Christmas party. You can read more about how they met in Chapter 14: Meeting People.

Moderately Less Frugal

Profile S-4: Slats and Marilyn

After running a successful insurance company for many years, Slats (yep, he's really tall) and Marilyn have enjoyed investing in fun things together—including a winter home in Florida and a summer home in North Carolina. After almost 60 years of marriage, their system has proven to work for them beautifully:

	Slats	Marilyn	Matrix Points:
Religion (importance: 1–4)	Christian—Presbyterian (1)	Christian—Presbyterian (1)	♥
Education	Bachelor's degree	Bachelor's degree	♥
Spending (1–4)	3	3	♥
Politics (1–4)	2	2	♥
Environment:			
▪ Birth Order	Firstborn of three	Firstborn of two	♥
▪ Clean (1–4)	2	2	♥
Chemistry	Type O	Type O	♥
Togetherness	Singing in the choir, classical music concerts, being with family, reading, public TV		♥
Matrix Score:			8

You could frame their Matrix! It's Ideal, with a score of 8. They consider themselves only mildly frugal, rating themselves both as 3s, but they've obviously invested well in their relationship and in everything else…as evidenced by their long-lasting marriage.

They have the full complement of matching RESPECT values and traits. They are equally Religious, Educated with bachelor's degrees, moderately Politically conservative, Firstborns and relatively fastidious (Environment), Type O blood Chemistry, and enjoy Togetherness with shared loves of music and family.

No wonder their marriage has lasted beyond a half of a century—there's very little they disagree about!

Profile S-5: Randy and Tammy

Tammy's father is a dentist, so she wasn't the least bit squeamish about marrying a veterinarian—she was very familiar with the medical field already. Tammy and Randy have been married for more than 20 years, and they share the same Spending approach:

	Randy	Tammy	Matrix Points:
Religion (importance: 1–4)	Christian—Presbyterian (2)	Christian—Presbyterian (2)	♥
Education	Doctorate	Bachelor's degree	♥
Spending (1–4)	3	3	♥
Politics (1–4)	1	2	♥
Environment:			
▪ Birth Order	Firstborn of four	Firstborn of four	♥
▪ Clean (1–4)	2	3	♥
Chemistry	Type A	Type A	♥
Togetherness	Dinners out, playing cards, watching videos and movies		♥
Matrix Score:			8

These two rate themselves as being on the moderately unfrugal side, though not completely unfrugal. The important thing is that they *interpret* their Spending habits as being basically the same. Just for the sake of argument, let's say their friends think they're actually quite tight with money. But that wouldn't matter: Others' opinions don't factor into the equation when it comes to compatibility—the important thing is how you think of yourself, and how you get along together.

The fact that they list "dinners out" as a favorite activity shows that they enjoy Spending their money on nice restaurants without feeling like they're wasting away their finances. On topics other than Spending, this couple wrote on their survey that Randy was raised Baptist, Tammy was raised Catholic, and they joined a Presbyterian church after getting married and going church-shopping together. They're also well aligned in the Chemistry and Birth Order factors, which further contribute to their common ground. They earn an Ideal score of 8 in the Matrix.

Profile S-6: Al and Vickie

Generally preferring to enjoy Spending their money without too much worry or guilt, Vickie and Al rate themselves on the less-strict side of the Spending spectrum, as you can see in their Matrix:

	Al	Vickie	Matrix Points:
Religion (importance: 1–4)	Christian—Methodist (2)	Christian—Methodist (2)	♥
Education	Some college	High school diploma	♥
Spending (1–4)	4	3	♥
Politics (1–4)	2	2	♥
Environment:			
▪ **Birth Order**	Lastborn of three (7 years younger than his next-oldest sibling)	Lastborn of three (12 years younger than her next-oldest sibling)	♥
▪ **Clean (1–4)**	2	3	♥
Chemistry	Type O	Type O	♥
Togetherness	Golf, fishing, gardening		♥
Matrix Score:			8

One thing you don't see in their Matrix is that they each experienced a family tragedy at almost identical ages while growing up: His brother passed away when Al was just 12, and her mother passed away when Vickie was only 13. There's no doubt that they therefore share certain similar perspectives as a result of these life-altering, family-changing events. (Read about a comparable story in Profile Env-Birth-7, Kevin and Kara, in the Environment chapter.)

On a lighter note, Vickie and Al have enjoyed fishing and playing golf together over the course of their 13 years of marriage. They are both moderately fastidious and moderately conservative. Plus, they are each the Lastborn of three, but both are unquestionably Virtual Firstborns with such enormous gaps: 12 and 7 years younger than their respective older siblings! They earn an Ideal score of 8, and I'm sure Al—who has since gone on to be with the Lord—is looking down from Heaven and smiling.

Final Thoughts on Spending...

Come payday, what do you do with your money? Do you like to sometimes just go wild and have fun, and worry about it later? Or do you approach it methodically and deliberately?

It's almost impossible to find two people who like to spend their money in exactly the same way, but you should find someone who has the same general Spending perspectives and values that you do. You know where you rated yourself on the 1–4 Spending scale in the beginning of this book, so try to find someone who is either the same or one "notch" away from you.

A classic wedding vow is "For richer or for poorer," in which you promise to stick together through all kinds of foreseen and unforeseen financial circumstances. If the two of you are generally like-minded in this arena, you will handle your money well together, and stay happy together, regardless of the financial situation.

~ Cheat Sheet ~	
RESPECT	**Answer:**
Spending (1–4)	...Look for someone who ranks themselves as the same or only one "notch" away from you

RESPECT

Chapter 6: Politics

What is your political bent?	1=Conservative; 4=Liberal: 1 2 3 4

> *"No one party can fool all the people all of the time.*
> *That's why we have two parties."*
> *— Bob Hope*

Why This Is Important

Religion and Politics are the two volatile issues that tend to evoke the most emotional responses and, potentially, outrage when two people disagree with each other. Your Religion involves your God-view (spiritual), and your Political bent involves your worldview. And even if you think you "don't really care" about Politics, you do have opinions regarding how much the government should give freely to people in various situations, how much leeway businesses should receive in terms of taxes or pollution regulation, and the importance of weaponry for defense.

In civilized modern-day society, there is no right or wrong party to belong to: If all people were members of the same party, the organization would have too much power and would become skewed too far in one direction, which isn't healthy. (We've learned that the hard way throughout history, whenever a country has had only one party.) Various political parties in a democratic country force balance upon each other, so the noblest policies are brought to the fore and the extremist policies are usually ignored.

In the United States, the Political spectrum comprises "liberal" thought to "conservative" thought. Liberals are heart-centered: They make sure the poor and weak aren't forgotten for the sake of everyone's individual prosperity; they emphasize peace and tolerance, sometimes to the point of fault. They're compassionate, and they like the idea of the government taking care of things so nothing and no one fall through the cracks. Conservatives are mind-centered: They make sure principles and standards aren't set aside for the sake of individual lifestyles; they emphasize self-reliance and pragmatism, sometimes to the point of fault. They're practical, and they like to make sure hard work and initiative are allowed and enabled to flourish.

In essence, conservatives ensure that their corner of the world doesn't become a quagmire of codependency, with the motivated folks doing all the work, feeding and clothing the "wake-me-at-noon" unmotivated. Liberals, on the other hand, make sure that their corner of the world doesn't become a luck-of-the-draw crapshoot, where the strong and sensible are the only ones who enjoy life at all.

These reasons are why there is truly no right or wrong Political perspective—the world needs both. It's a healthy tension. But loyalties and values are important, and that's why this should ideally be closely aligned in a marriage.

The big picture is largely community responsibility versus personal responsibility, because governmental policies either affect and protect freedom (personal responsibility) or they aim to ensure equal treatment of everyone regardless of individual effort (community responsibility). Our perspectives on these issues come from our own experiences.

The Goal

Who you're most compatible with: In Politics—just like in Spending—it's best to be the same number or only one "notch" away from the other person on the 1–4 Politics scale.

You and Mr/s. Right need to be either the same number on the 1–4 scale, or only one notch apart. If you and your mate are two or all three notches away from each other on this scale of 1 to 4, dinner-table talk during election season could become difficult due to this issue's tendency to be splashed everywhere in the media and dominant in intellectual conversations.

If you've really fallen for someone, you may rationalize that you can just avoid discussing the hot-button issue(s) that you two disagree on—but eventually, it will be brought up. (We'll discuss one famous exception to this rule, James Carville and Mary Matalin, later in this chapter.) It's best to discuss this topic while you're still dating, to understand and respect each other on general Political issues before you get to the point of tying the knot.

The best approach is to bring it up gently, while your bellies are full (we're all happier when we've had dinner!) and you're not around other people. It's not as easy to be frank if one or both of you feel that others might overhear the conversation, even if it is among strangers. Decide beforehand that you're going to discuss it rationally, with a true intent of seeing the other person's perspective. If your goal is to convince the other person that you're right and they're wrong, the relationship will probably not work.

Here we'll meet some couples who demonstrate how being in agreement Politically is a very relevant factor in compatibility.

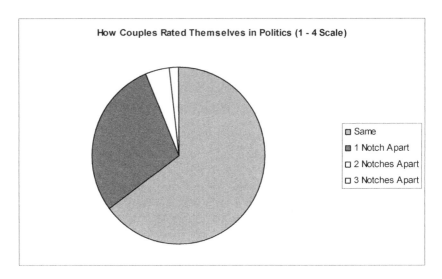

Figure P-1: Overall Matrix Study Results of Political Tendencies in Marriage

Politically Liberal or Somewhat Liberal

Profile P-1: Harry and Mary

I was thrilled to receive this couple's survey, because Harry is a retired U.S. Congressman—and as it turns out, they have a Perfect score of 7 on the Matrix scale. Naturally, someone who is as involved in Politics as Harry will want to find someone who agrees Politically, and he found a wonderful match in Mary.

Most survey respondents rated themselves as 2 or 3 in the 1–4 range, preferring to peg themselves as fairly moderate. But those who rated themselves as 1 or 4 usually were married to someone on the **same side** of the spectrum—i.e., 1&1 or 1&2 on the conservative side, or 3&4 or 4&4 on the liberal side. Mary and Harry have been married for more than 50 years, and here is their Matrix:

54

	Harry	Mary	Matrix Points:
Religion (importance: 1–4)	Christian—Presbyterian	Christian—Presbyterian (1)	♥
Education	Master's degree	Bachelor's degree	♥
Spending (1–4)	2	1	♥
Politics (1–4)	4	4	♥
Environment:			
▪ **Birth Order**	Second of three (3 years younger than his next-oldest sibling)	Firstborn of two	♥
▪ **Clean (1–4)**	3	2	♥
Chemistry	(not available)	(not available)	–
Togetherness	Movies, tennis, travel, family get-togethers		♥
Matrix Score:			7

Their Matrix also shows how even if two people don't know their blood types, which describes a surprising number of people, you can still evaluate the relationship fairly well using the Matrix scale.

Profile P-2: Tom and Ann

Both ordained Presbyterian ministers, Ann and Tom share plenty of interests and perspectives, and they both labeled themselves as very liberal on the Politics scale. In answering the Togetherness question, Tom wrote "Voting" as an activity he particularly enjoys, so he obviously finds it important! So this high value on Politics makes it almost imperative that Ann shares his views in this arena. Here is their Matrix:

	Tom	Ann	Matrix Points:
Religion (importance: 1–4)	Christian— Presbyterian (1)	Christian— Presbyterian (1)	♥
Education	Master's degree	Master's degree	♥
Spending (1–4)	2	3	♥
Politics (1–4)	4	4	♥
Environment:			
▪ **Birth Order**	Second of three (3 years younger than his next-oldest sibling)	Firstborn of two	♥
▪ **Clean (1–4)**	3	1	–
Chemistry	Type A	Type O	–
Togetherness	Church, movies, TV, reading, dinner, vacations, seeing friends, voting		♥
Professional Extra Credit	Both are Presbyterian ministers		♥
Matrix Score:			7

Ann and Tom are largely compatible across the board, especially in Religion, Education, Spending, Politics, and Togetherness. Tom's upbringing as a Middle-Child enables them to automatically satisfy one of the two Environment factors (Birth Order), as Ann is the Firstborn of two. (If she had been an Only-Child or a Twin, though, they wouldn't have earned this Matrix point.) Although they're disparate in Cleanliness and in Chemistry, their shared professional commonalities give them Professional Extra Credit which helps make up for it—just like Marcus and Sandra in Profile S-3 (in the Spending chapter).

On the back of their survey, Ann and Tom wrote: "We love discovering new things about each other, which still happens frequently." And after more than 45 years of marriage, you can take their example to the bank...or to the voting booth.

Profile P-3: Phil and Suzanne

This Generation-X couple enjoy putting their creative juices to work on their home-based advertising business, which they work on together during their free time. They also both rate themselves as moderately liberal on the Politics scale in their Matrix:

	Phil	Suzanne	Matrix Points:
Religion (importance: 1–4)	Christian— Catholic (3)	Christian— Catholic (3)	♥
Education	Bachelor's degree	Bachelor's degree	♥
Spending (1–4)	3	2	♥
Politics (1–4)	3	3	♥
Environment:			
▪ **Birth Order**	Only-Child	Firstborn of two	♥
▪ **Clean (1–4)**	1	2	♥
Chemistry	Type O	Type O	♥
Togetherness	Walking, traveling, shopping, working on our freelance ad business		♥
Professional Extra Credit	Both in the advertising field		♥
Matrix Score:			9

Wow—they are one of only a few couples in this study who actually score an "über-ideal" 9 on their Matrix. In addition to corresponding Political views, Suzanne and Phil match up just right in every arena: Catholic, bachelor's degrees, moderately frugal, Firstborns, relatively fastidious, Type O, and plenty of different activities they enjoy doing together. Note that Phil is a "super-Firstborn" as an Only-Child, so this matches very well with Suzanne's upbringing as the Firstborn in her family.

They're only one notch apart in the Spending and Cleanliness areas, which is perfectly acceptable—in fact, it's good that they have a few slight differences, otherwise they might be too much alike!

Politically Moderate or Independent

Profile P-4: Dallas and Joan

On their survey, Dallas didn't choose from the 1–4 range for the Politics question, because he's a Libertarian—generally, socially liberal and fiscally conservative. Joan described herself as a 2, which is a moderate stance and can therefore be agreeable with his non-conformist Political views. They have been married for more than 20 years, and here is their Matrix:

	Dallas	Joan	Matrix Points:
Religion (importance: 1–4)	Christian— Catholic (2)	Christian— Episcopalian (1)	♥
Education	Juris doctorate	Some college (Associate's degree)	–
Spending (1–4)	4	4	♥
Politics (1–4)	(abstain)	2	♥
Environment:			
▪ Birth Order	Only-Child	Firstborn of two	♥
▪ Clean (1–4)	1	2	♥
Chemistry	Type O	Type B	♥
Togetherness	Visiting old bookstores, watching TV, eating, reading, flying, sightseeing, hiking		♥
Matrix Score:			7

Glancing through their Matrix, you can see that they match up very well in Religion, Spending, Politics, Environment (both Birth Order and Cleanliness), Chemistry, and Togetherness, with their only disparate spot being in Education. They have a Perfect score of 7.

This couple live away from the city in a place where deer come and feed in their backyard. They have several cats whom they adore as children, and they even try their best to avoid killing indoor bugs—insects that come into their home are carefully gathered and taken outside. They truly treasure God's creation with the utmost respect and love, and this same respect and love are easily seen in their marriage as well.

Dallas and Joan are a shining example of how day-to-day tendencies and values are reflected in other areas of one's life. You can get a pretty good idea of how a person will act in a marriage based on how they treat other people.

Politically Conservative or Somewhat Conservative

Profile P-5: Dick and Tootsie

Tootsie's and Dick's rating of themselves as both 2s, or moderately conservative on the Politics scale, represents the mathematical "mode" of the survey's participating couples: More than 27% of the couples who answered this question labeled themselves as both 2s, which is a higher percentage than any of the other combinations (1&1, 3&4, etc.).

This high rate of moderate conservatives in this survey is most likely due to the fact that marriage is indeed a traditional institution, and traditionalists tend toward somewhat conservative thinking. Also, people who are somewhat easygoing—and are thus easy to get along with in relationships—are largely empathetic with others, which makes for a more moderate viewpoint. So it makes sense that so many of the survey participants ranked themselves as 2s on the Politics scale.

	Dick	Tootsie	Matrix Points:
Religion (im-portance: 1–4)	Christian—Presbyterian (1)	Christian—Presbyterian (1)	♥
Education	Master's degree	Some college	–
Spending (1–4)	2	3	♥
Politics (1–4)	2	2	♥
Environment:			
▪ **Birth Order**	Lastborn of two (4 years younger than his older sibling)	Third of five (2 years younger than her next-oldest sibling)	♥
▪ **Clean (1–4)**	2	1	♥
Chemistry	Type O	Type O	♥
Togetherness	Traveling, gardening, visiting with grandchildren and family and friends		♥
Matrix Score:			7

In addition to a shared Political philosophy, they consider themselves very religious, moderately frugal, and fairly neat-and-clean. Plus, her status as a Middle-Child makes her a great match for a Lastborn like Dick. They also share the same Chemistry and lots of favorite Togetherness activities. After more than 20 years of marriage, their like-mindedness proves to demonstrate the ultimate in a happy, successful marriage.

Profile P-6: Ken and Janie

Whereas most of the Presbyterians in this study are affiliated with the Presbyterian Church (U.S.A.), which tends to be generally more moderate in its political stances, Janie and Ken are members of the conservative Presbyterian Church in America (PCA). She grew up in the P.C. (USA), but they switched to the PCA denomination where they feel the more conservative principles are emphasized. Still, there's something to be said for the idea that church-going is and of itself a conservative habit—after all, the word "conservative" literally means traditional, prudent, and favoring preservation of (conserving) the existing order—so attending regular worship services fits neatly into that framework.

Not all religious people consider them selves conservative ("Exhibit A" of this is Profile P-2, Reverends Tom and Ann, earlier in this chapter), but almost all of them would likely admit to having some traditional values. You don't see very many grandparents who have been living together for decades without having been married to each other. And hopefully this trend will continue as it has for millennia.

Janie and Ken have been married for more than 10 years, and they describe themselves as being on the conservative end of the Political spectrum. Here is their Matrix:

	Ken	Janie	Matrix Points:
Religion (importance: 1–4)	Christian— Presbyterian (1)	Christian— Presbyterian (1)	♥
Education	Bachelor's degree	Bachelor's degree	♥
Spending (1–4)	2	3	♥
Politics (1–4)	2	1	♥
Environment:			
▪ Birth Order	Only-Child	Only-Child	♥
▪ Clean (1–4)	2	3	♥
Chemistry	Type O	Type O	♥
Togetherness	Exercising, playing games, reading, walking on the beach		♥
Matrix Score:			8

Janie and Ken are both educated with bachelor's degrees, both are Only-Children, both are Type Os, and both are moderate in the areas of Spending and Cleanliness. And they have plenty of low-maintenance Togetherness avocations as well. How hard is it to sit down and read some good books and magazines together in the same room? Or to hop in the car on a Saturday and take an enjoyable walk together along the local beach? This is the stuff that makes for a great marriage.

The Elephant in the Room (The Couple You Were Thinking About)

Profile P-7: James Carville and Mary Matalin

The quintessential exception to this rule about Politics is Mary Matalin and James Carville, the 1992 U.S. presidential campaign strategists for (respectively) President George H. W. Bush, the Republican candidate up for re-election, and Arkansas Governor (and subsequently President) Bill Clinton, the Democratic candidate.

Mary and James continue to be happily married at the time of this writing. Based on public information, their Matrix can be pieced together:

	James	Mary	Matrix Points:
Religion (importance: 1–4)	Christian—Catholic	Christian—Catholic	♥
Education	Juris doctorate (law school)	Juris doctorate (law school)	♥
Spending (1–4)	(From a working-class family, now a highly successful Washington, D.C., consultant)	(From a working-class family, now a highly successful Washington, D.C., consultant)	♥
Politics (1–4)	3 or 4	1 or 2	–
Environment:			
▪ **Birth Order**	Firstborn	Firstborn	♥
▪ **Clean (1–4)**	(not available)	(not available)	
Chemistry	(not available)	(not available)	♥*
Togetherness	Running, working out, food/wine aficionados		♥
Professional Extra Credit	Both are political consultants		♥
Matrix Score:			7+

"If we talked politics we'd just have these screaming fights, so we avoided the obvious areas of conflict and found that just about everywhere else we were simpatico," said Mary in their book *All's Fair: Love, War, and*

Running for President. "My original attraction to James was that he was a guy doing something that I loved in a way that was different than I'd ever seen it done…. Politics is a passion…. And your mate has to get it…. It's hard to be companionable and compatible with somebody who's not in the business."

"We were so excited because we really did like each other," said James.[2]

*…And all this is why I gave them a point for Chemistry—you can just hear the excitement in their voices over their attraction, even after many years of marriage.

So there you have it. Politics itself is a love they share, even though the issues involved aren't in agreement. From the very beginning, they were physically attracted to each other, shared similar backgrounds, and shared almost all of the same values—and they have an incredible, deep-seated *respect* for each other.

Soon after the untimely death of NBC's "Meet the Press" host Tim Russert, the network invited regular guests Carville and Matalin to come and contribute their fond memories about the late anchor. Sitting in chairs next to each other, these two broke into sobs over the loss of their friend. It was an amazing moment that, in a surprising way, showed how similar these two are to each other on a personal level, despite their Political differences.

Tying the knot under such severe circumstances is unusual and not for the faint of heart, but this couple exemplifies how the basics must match and how you have to develop strategies to avoid arguments if there is a mismatched area.

On James Carville's and Mary Matalin's Matrix, although we don't know their Chemistry or Cleanliness traits, we do know that they are both Firstborns from working-class families when growing up. They're both Catholic, and they both have juris doctorates from law school.

As demonstrated by Mary and James, if there is too much disagreement on the Politics issue but you're otherwise "simpatico," you will probably need to just avoid the issue altogether in conversation—there are plenty of other things to talk about in life! Determine the level of tolerance and respect for each other's opinions on this issue before you venture forward in a relationship.

Final Thoughts on Politics...

The Politics factor is important in compatibility because basic beliefs, perspectives, and values are as **broad** as what quantifies as true wisdom—i.e., is your idea of a wise leader someone who leads from pure intelligence thanks to high education, or someone who has proven to make good decisions from gut-level insight?—and they are as **focused** as what the proper qualities of a leader should be...and, therefore, the qualities you probably want to emulate.

Each side of the Political spectrum tends to find certain extreme viewpoints of the opposing side as morally offensive, and this is why Politics is a value—indeed, a worldview—that can't be ignored when looking for Mr/s. Right.

~ Cheat Sheet ~	
RESPECT	**Answer:**
Political bent (1–4)	...Look for someone who ranks themselves as the same or only one "notch" away from you

RESPECT

Chapter 7: Environment

This category is twofold:
(1) *Family* Environment (Birth Order)...

What is your birth order (i.e., your role in the family environment)?	☐ Only-Child ☐ Firstborn of ___ (how many?) ☐ Middle child, number ___ of ___ (how many?); my next-oldest sibling was ___ years older than I, and my next-youngest sibling was ___ years younger than I ☐ Lastborn of ___ (how many?); my next-oldest sibling was ___ years older than I

...and (2) *Surroundings* Environment (Cleanliness):

How important to you are neat-and-clean surroundings?	1=Very important; 4=Not very important: 1 2 3 4

Part 1: *Family* Environment (Birth Order)

When my Mom was in her mid-20s, she read a magazine article about compatibility. But after reading it, "I had decided I wasn't going to get married," she said.

"[The article] said how you have to have ALL these things in common for a marriage to really work out. It said if you come from a big family, you should marry somebody from a big family."

64

The article also suggested that people of the same Birth Order tend to get along and relate to each other the best. But she was the oldest of seven kids (and grew up on a farm), so this advice seemed to be a tall order. "Well, about six months after reading that article, I met Bob."

Bob (my Dad) was the oldest of seven kids, too (and grew up on a farm). And everything else matched up beautifully as well, not just their unusual Birth Order. They've been married for over 40 years.

Why This Is Important

Your Birth Order deeply affects how you perceive your role in relationships with other people. This perception is established at a young age: You quickly learn if your best strategy in gaining attention—and getting what you want from your parents—is by being responsible (generally a Firstborn/Only Child trait), cute (generally a Lastborn trait), or adaptable (generally a Middle-Child trait).

The Goal

Who you're most compatible with: *In Birth Order, if you're…*
…an Only-Child, you're highly compatible with an Only-Child, Firstborn, or Virtual Firstborn
…a Firstborn, you're highly compatible with anyone except a true Lastborn (but you are compatible with a Lastborn who is a Virtual Firstborn)
…a Middle-Child, you're highly compatible with anyone except an Only-Child or a Twin
…a Lastborn, you're highly compatible with anyone except a Firstborn or Only-Child
…a Twin, you're highly compatible with anyone except a Middle-Child

You are most compatible with others of your same Birth Order as well as those who grew up in certain other roles—and you are less compatible with others. Think about it: If you grew up being able to pick on or be better at things than your little brother, you will most closely identify with those who also have this bit of a superiority complex! Or, if you grew up in the middle of several siblings, you will most value others who can keep everyone together and not rock the boat just like you did naturally when you were growing up.

But there are nuances to these and the other roles, and these nuances are explained in this chapter. Your role in the family in which you were raised strongly influences how much confidence you have in certain situations as well as the role you assume in relationships and in groups, and this directly translates into how you relate to other people for the rest of your life.

However, there are exceptions to the Birth Order rule. Your Birth Order is only a guide for what your role in the family was; there may be extenuating circumstances that make your own Birth Order inconsequential as far as your role. Having an older sibling who has disabilities, having siblings who came into the family by a parent remarrying, or having older siblings who are about five or more years older than you can affect how you perceive the world around you and how you deal with everyone. If you did have special familial circumstances, your perceptions may be quite different from others who otherwise match your "technical" Birth Order.

"Virtual" Birth Order

A well-known psychological phenomenon is the 5-Year Difference Rule, which is this: **If you were about 5 or more years younger than your next-oldest sibling, you were likely raised as a Virtual Firstborn,** so you will tend to be most compatible with Firstborns, Only-Children, and those whose Birth Order matches yours (i.e., if you're a Middle-Child or Lastborn).

The reason you're like a Firstborn is because you weren't competing for the same kind of attention from your parents as your older sibling(s), and you may have almost felt like you had three (or more) parent-figures rather than siblings. Along the same lines, if you were 5 or more years older than your next-youngest sibling, your relationship with that sibling is different than if you were closer in age.

(Several participants wrote "4.5 years apart" on their surveys, so I allowed that to be rounded up to 5 years for this purpose—no need to be too legalistic about it.)

Another reason for the 5-Year Difference Rule is that an older sibling usually feels compelled to act as a mentor for a younger sibling; this mentoring relationship is even stronger with a greater age gap, because the older sibling has learned so much more than the younger sibling, so why not help the brother or sister avoid the same stupid mistakes? This "leadership" behavior is more easily accepted by a younger sibling the larger the age gap between the two, because the natural feeling of competition is diminished.

There are other ways in which you might be a Virtual Firstborn. You may technically be a Middle-Child, but the Firstborn died as an infant, so you never knew that person. Therefore, you never had an older sibling chiding you or doing things first, so you didn't grow up with the same perceptions as someone who did.

Similarly, if you were adopted and raised as an Only-Child, you are an Only-Child for our purposes here regardless of whether you technically had siblings by your birth parents, because you identify with that role. But if you were raised with cousins or other children in the same household, your role in the family Environment is based on your age difference as compared with those other children. Your role may also be influenced by how your parents (or guardians) treated you, if it was a blended family. If you were raised as a Firstborn until age 7, then a parent remarried and you thus gained an older step-sibling, you may have a combination of perspectives and attitudes from these experiences.

One fascinating finding that has been discovered relatively recently at the time of this writing is the fact that, if a man was the **first male** born in the family, it's very likely he grew up with a bit of a Virtual Firstborn experience. This phenomenon explains why you may meet a very confident man who acts like a Firstborn but isn't, and he is likely a Middle-Child or Lastborn with older sisters but no older brothers.

Firstborns and Compatibility

Classic traits:
- Confident
- Quick to take charge
- Somewhat bossy

If you were a Firstborn, you probably picked on your younger sibling(s) but didn't have to worry about physical retribution until your teens, if at all. This experience makes Firstborns more apt to take charge, more bullyish, and generally more confident in social situations than those in the other roles. Firstborns feel the need to always be right, be in charge (even if it's over a small realm of something), and have the last word.

They also tend to identify more with the parents, because they have, or at least *feel* like they have, more responsibility than the younger siblings. This role is especially evident when they have to babysit younger siblings or cousins. Firstborns may even help their parents change diapers at a young age, which is an extremely adult activity. They may help their parents set the dinner table while the younger siblings play. Such adult activities make Firstborns' confidence level soar!

Firstborns grow up knowing more and understanding more than their siblings at any given point, simply because they're older and naturally have learned more information in life than their younger peers. They get frustrated when they see younger siblings or cousins making mistakes that they've already learned from, and that's when the bullying tendency rears its head. "Don't do that! That's wrong!"

The oh-so-cuteness factor of younger siblings creates a natural differentiation of roles, so Firstborns quickly realize that they can please their parents by being responsible and by helping their little brother or sister. As per basic survival instincts, we all develop strategies to gain what we want, and everyone wants to be loved and accepted. But these strategies—which become habits—differ among the various Birth Order types. So they relate to others differently, sometimes in downright opposite ways.

The Goal

Firstborns get along best with other Firstborns and Only-Children; they also get along very well with Middle-Children and with Lastborns whose next-oldest siblings were 5 or more years older, thus rendering them Virtual Firstborns.

Firstborns are literally born into the family role: They are expected to be leaders, more mature than their younger siblings (regardless of the Firstborn's age, because it's always relative), to accept responsibility for younger children when parents aren't around, and to make good decisions. They feel much more pressure from the parents to behave with maturity, and they usually get along very well with their parents because they identify with having responsibility.

Firstborns and "true" Lastborns are least likely to get married to each other. This can be attributed to the fact that Firstborns and Lastborns have opposite tendencies, and thus completely different perspectives regarding their role in a family and how to best get along with others. Lastborns often perceive Firstborns as being bullyish and inflexible, and Firstborns may perceive Lastborns as being immature and prone to tantrums (unless they're Virtual Firstborns).

In some of the Birth Order pie charts in this chapter, I'm separating out the Virtual Firstborns as a class unto themselves; and although these folks are technically either Middle-Children or Lastborns, they are considered only Virtual Firstborns for our purposes here.

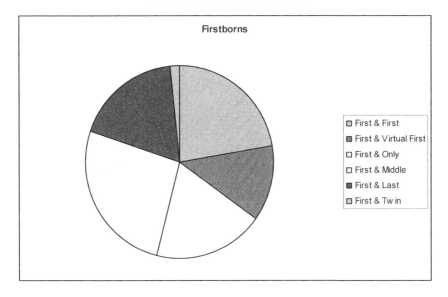

Figure Env-Birth-1: Matrix Study Results of Firstborns' Tendencies in Marriage

Profile Env-Birth-1: David and Lucy

A prime example of demonstrating the leadership qualities and self-reliance common to Firstborns are this couple, who regularly fulfill requests whenever help is needed. After being married more than 40 years, Lucy and David's Matrix says it all:

	David	Lucy	Matrix Points:
Religion (importance: 1–4)	Christian— Presbyterian (1)	Christian— Presbyterian (1)	♥
Education	High school diploma	Some college	♥
Spending (1–4)	2	1	♥
Politics (1–4)	1	1	♥
Environment:			
▪ **Birth Order**	Firstborn of two	Firstborn of two	♥
▪ **Clean (1–4)**	2	2	♥
Chemistry	Type B	Type O	♥
Togetherness	Traveling, walking		♥
Matrix Score:			8

Lucy and David match perfectly across the board—plus, they're both early risers and take a walk together around their neighborhood every morning. They are active leaders in their church, and they usually unlock the church's doors first thing Sunday morning and get the coffee pot started for everyone. Such initiative and reliability are typical of Firstborns, and a non-Firstborn who intends to marry a Firstborn will do well to understand the role that person will assume naturally in relationships. And as you can see, they match up incredibly well all around and thus earn an Ideal score of 8.

Subset of Firstborns: Virtual Firstborns

As explained earlier, Virtual Firstborns are Middle-Children or Lastborns who are about 5 or more years younger than their next-oldest sibling. Compatibility-wise, Virtual Firstborns have amazing flexibility—they get along very well with true Firstborns as well as with those of their own true Birth Order. In fact, because of this, a Middle-Child who is actually a Virtual Firstborn is compatible with people of **all** Birth Order types, because this sort of Middle-Child can indeed be compatible with an Only-Child.

Profile Env-Birth-2: Marshall and Miriam

As the Middle-Child of three who is 7 years younger than his older sister, Marshall is rendered as a Virtual Firstborn—which is a quality that matches up excellently with Firstborn Miriam. He was too much younger than his older sister for there to be much rivalry with her, so instead he grew up more like a Firstborn. After almost 60 years of marriage, their Matrix speaks volumes:

	Marshall	Miriam	Matrix Points:
Religion (importance: 1–4)	Christian— Episcopalian (1)	Christian— Episcopalian (1)	♥
Education	Bachelor's degree	Some college	♥
Spending (1–4)	2	3	♥
Politics (1–4)	1	1	♥
Environment:			
▪ **Birth Order**	Second of three (7 years younger than his next-oldest sibling)	Firstborn of two	♥
▪ **Clean (1–4)**	2	1	♥
Chemistry	Type O	Type O	♥
Togetherness	Reading, watching TV, golf, snorkeling, swimming, conversations, cribbage, being together		♥
Matrix Score:			8

They're exemplary match-ups in every category, and they could have been a featured profile for any of the RESPECT chapters in this book. Marshall wrote this on the back of his survey:

"I first laid eyes on Miriam when she was 13. She was living with her grandparents on the same street as a close friend of mine. I distinctly remember remarking, to a friend of mine, Harry Bell, 'There goes the kind of girl you marry!'"

There's no need for us to lose the childlike romantic innocence Marshall displays as a member of the World War II generation. The modern reaction to his statement might be a bit cynical or critical, but rest assured— his words are the stuff of the jubilation that lasts a lifetime. Although he and Miriam endured their share of tough times, this transcendent love has surpassed it all.

Only-Children and Compatibility

Classic traits:

- Confident
- Get along best with others who are confident
- Don't naturally blend with groups or share attention

Only-Children grow up as the focal point of the family, and all the attention (as well as the pressure to succeed and make the adults proud) is on them. They therefore grow up as "super-Firstborns." They don't have younger siblings with whom they must compete for attention and admiration from adults, so they learn to communicate in very adult ways. Their parents *are* their peers in the home, so Only-Children usually have high maturity levels.

Because they matured so quickly, Only-Children have the tendency to be self-absorbed and have difficulty putting others' needs before their own. They often lack certain cooperation skills learned (by necessity) by those who do have siblings, but they react so favorably to adults' admonition that they have a social escape route if peer cooperation is a problem later in life.

The Goal

Only-Children rated highest in compatibility on the Matrix survey with Firstborns, as is pathetically obvious in the below figure!

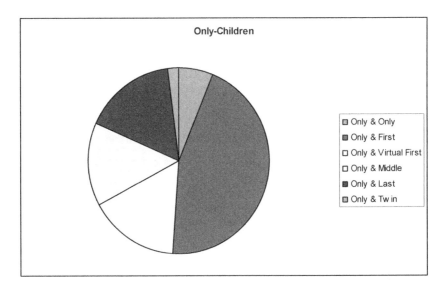

Figure Env-Birth-2: Matrix Study Results of Only-Children's Tendencies in Marriage

Isn't that fascinating: A full 67% of Only-Children were married to other Only-Children, Firstborns, or Virtual Firstborns. They tend to strongly identify with their Birth Order status, probably more than any of the other types, so they do seek out those who have similar leadership-style and independent perspectives.

Profile Env-Birth-3: Donald and Charlotte

As an Only-Child and a Firstborn, respectively, Donald and Charlotte share a lot of self-reliance and confidence. They have an Ideal Matrix, with a score of 8. And after a whopping 65 years of marriage, this couple deserves the attention of anyone trying to solve the puzzle of lifelong compatibility!

One thing I noticed among participating couples was that the longer the marriage, the stronger the similarities. Charlotte and Donald match each other perfectly (with an acceptable one-notch difference in Spending). Bottom line: A couple will "gel" over the years and become more similar to each other as their love deepens and matures. Here is their Matrix:

	Donald	Charlotte	Matrix Points:
Religion (importance: 1–4)	Christian— Presbyterian (1)	Christian— Presbyterian (1)	♥
Education	Doctorate	Bachelor's degree	♥
Spending (1–4)	1	2	♥
Politics (1–4)	1	1	♥
Environment:			
▪ **Birth Order**	Only-Child	Firstborn of four	♥
▪ **Clean (1–4)**	2	2	♥
Chemistry	Type O	Type B	♥
Togetherness	Dancing, reading, watching tennis on TV, listening to music		♥
Matrix Score:			8

It was interesting to compare Matrix survey results between couples who had been married only a year against longstanding marriages like Donald and Charlotte's, because the longer the marriage, the closer and more obvious the similarities were on paper. Over time in a strong marriage, the couple will develop a greater appreciation for each other's interests and talents. And the reason their bond grows stronger is that they already have a strong foundation of similar shared values and backgrounds.

The great part about that process is that you don't even really notice it's happening! Time has a way of smoothing us over—just like older stones are smooth after being refined over time, yet newer stones have sharp edges—likewise, we humans become refined over time. Each spouse has natural or learned talents, and because of their relationship together, they will each become a smoother, more refined version of themselves than they would be otherwise.

Middle-Children and Compatibility

Classic traits:
- Can blend well with others and not disturb
- Great team players
- May lack confidence

Middle-children are often the best at showing nonjudgmental empathy to others and at listening attentively, and they are usually the most humble and (sometimes) the most anxious of all the Birth Order types. They also tend to have the least amount of confidence, because they were outperformed by their older siblings and "out-cuted" by their younger siblings. Therefore, Middle-Children learn to impress their parents by being agreeable and differentiating themselves from their siblings in that important way. Their humbleness is an admirable trait which the others often try to emulate, especially as adults.

As far as their role in the family, the 5-Year Difference Rule applies more thoroughly to Middle-Children than to anyone else. If you were raised as a Middle-Child but your next-oldest sibling is about 5 or more years older than you, then you may actually have many Firstborn-like tendencies and perspectives. This is because you didn't have to compete for the same kind of attention as your next-oldest sibling—when you were 6, that sibling was 11 or older—which makes for more of a mentor-child relationship than a peer-peer relationship.

Similarly, if you're a Middle-Child but your next-youngest sibling is 5 or more years *younger* than you, you may identify as much with a Lastborn as you do with another Middle-Child. You were probably picked on and teased by your older siblings, but you also may have had to help change diapers or babysit your younger siblings like a Firstborn. So, it's a little complicated, but it boils down to the role you most closely identify with.

The Goal

This is the most versatile of the Birth Order types. The survey's results demonstrate that Middle-Children are incredibly flexible when it comes to compatibility with other Birth Order types: Of the 94 couples in which one or both spouses were Middle-Children, 19% were Middle-and-Middle, 34% were Middle-and-Lastborn, 37% were Middle-and-Firstborn, and about 10% were Middle-and-Only-Children. Their compatibility with Firstborns and Only-Children is stronger if their own next-oldest sibling is 5 or more years older in age.

Middle-Children are equal-opportunity folks: They can identify with Firstborns, because they, too, had younger siblings whom they probably picked on; they can identify with Lastborns, because they were probably picked on themselves by their older siblings; and they obviously relate well to fellow Middle-Children. Their compatibility with Only-Children is lowest because, naturally, an Only-Child is accustomed to being the *center* of attention most of the time—whereas a Middle-Child is accustomed to having to *share* the attention most of the time.

In the following pie chart, the Virtual Firstborn phenomenon has been removed in order to show Middle-Children in their true colors.

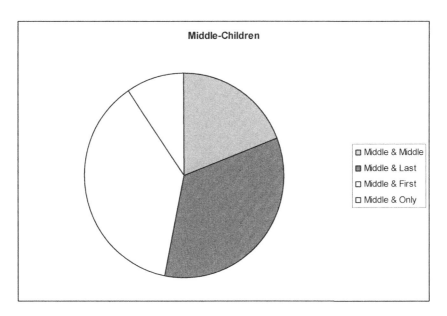

Figure Env-Birth-3: Matrix Study Results of Middle-Children's Tendencies in Marriage

Profile Env-Birth-4: Milt and Helen

Having surpassed their golden anniversary, Milt and Helen are both Middle-Children who have been married for 54 years. Although Middle-Children are the most versatile of all Birth Order types (as far as compatibility with other types), they certainly have most in common with fellow Middle-Children.

"Growing up as one of ten children, there was no other option than to be agreeable, congenial, harmonious, and noncontradictory," says Helen. "All of this helped to prepare me for college life, married life, parenthood, and generally getting along in the world."

Helen's self-analysis is a quintessential summary of why Middle-Children *are* so compatible with Firstborns, Lastborns, and their fellow Middle-Children. When growing up, Middle-Children develop strategies to get along with everyone, so they are naturally flexible and agreeable. The Firstborn in Helen's household would probably have a somewhat different perspective of the family dynamic, describing his or her relationships with siblings a little differently—there would probably be words like "helper" and "responsibility" rather than the words Helen used above. Here is their Matrix:

	Milt	Helen	Matrix Points:
Religion (importance: 1–4)	Christian (1)	Christian (1)	♥
Education	Bachelor's degree	Bachelor's degree	♥
Spending (1–4)	2	1	♥
Politics (1–4)	1	1	♥
Environment:			
▪ **Birth Order**	Third of four (5 years younger than his next-oldest sibling)	Sixth of 10 (2 years younger than her next-oldest sibling)	♥
▪ **Clean (1–4)**	1	1	♥
Chemistry	Type O	Type O	♥
Togetherness	Golf, dancing		♥
Matrix Score:			8

Milt is a Virtual Firstborn, but the fact that he's indeed a Middle-Child makes him highly compatible with anyone except Twins and Only-Children—and he's Ideally compatible with the ever-agreeable, ever-harmonious Helen.

Profile Env-Birth-5: Joel and Jane

These adaptable and friendly Middle-Children found each other while vacationing with friends in Greece. While still in college, Jane went on vacation to Greece with her sisters. In the meantime, Joel was in the U.S. Navy, and his ship made a stop in Greece. When he and his buddies and she and her sisters were milling about, the two groups noticed each other, started talking, and realized that they were all from the United States. Jane and Joel have been together ever since, and they're both teachers in Minnesota.

In addition to both being Middle-Children, everything else falls neatly into place in their Matrix as well. After more than 30 years of marriage, Jane and Joel's Matrix helps explain what keeps them together:

	Joel	Jane	Matrix Points:
Religion (importance: 1–4)	Christian— Lutheran (1)	Christian— Lutheran (1)	♥
Education	Master's degree	Master's degree	♥
Spending (1–4)	2	3	♥
Politics (1–4)	3	2/3	♥
Environment:			
▪ Birth Order	Second of three (5 years younger than his older sibling)	Fourth of seven (3 years younger than her next-oldest sibling)	♥
▪ Clean (1–4)	2	2	♥
Chemistry	Type AB	Type A	♥
Togetherness	Traveling, eating out, walking the dog, watching TV news, talking politics		♥
Matrix Score:			8

The moral of their story is that you truly never know when, where, or how you will meet Mr. or Mrs. Right—and that even Americans can find their Ideal match in Greece or anywhere else. So keep your eyes open even when you're on vacation.

Profile Env-Birth-6: Doug and Carole

A classic example of a Middle-Child marrying a Lastborn, Carole and Doug have an Ideal Matrix—and after more than 15 years of marriage, they have found each other to be their own ideal match-up.

Both in artistic professions, they share the same wavelength and deep-seated respect and appreciation for each other's vocations. The only thing that's a bit off is the importance they each place on Religion; however, they are of the same religious faith background, so they do share that common understanding and basic belief system. Everything else matches beautifully. Here is their Matrix:

	Doug	Carole	Matrix Points:
Religion (importance: 1–4)	Christian (3)	Christian (1)	♥
Education	High school diploma	Some college	♥
Spending (1–4)	3	3	♥
Politics (1–4)	2	2	♥
Environment:			
▪ Birth Order	Second of three (2 years younger than his older sibling)	Lastborn of five (1 year younger than her next-oldest sibling)	♥
▪ Clean (1–4)	2	2	♥
Chemistry	Type AB	Type A	♥
Togetherness	Eating together, hanging out, traveling		♥
Matrix Score:			8

Carole and Doug maintain close relationships with their siblings and other family members; they also enjoy remodeling and fixing up their home, and going away on the weekends.

Your goal is to find a kind, trustworthy person who shares similar values and goals as you have, just as Carole and Doug have found matching qualities in each other.

Lastborns and Compatibility

Classic traits:
- Charming and disarming
- Get along by being and/or acting "cute"
- May be somewhat whiny

And then there are the "babies"! Lastborns learn to be most effective and get what they want by being cute. They're naturally adorable because of their relatively small size, as compared to their older siblings, so adults will swoon at the littlest one. "Oh, you're so CUTE!" is a phrase that a Lastborn can keenly relate to. This strategy stays with them throughout their adult lives, and they can go into "cute mode" at will in order to gain friends or get along with others.

Lastborns also learn to cry to get what they want, and this can translate into a whiny tendency as an adult. They grow up being teased and picked on by their older siblings; to deal with this, if they had more than one older sibling, Lastborns might have even latched onto an older sibling—especially if that sibling is 5 or more years older in age—so there would be a defender.

But if the Lastborn's next-oldest sibling was 5 or more years older, then the Lastborn may have been raised with the perspectives of an Only-Child and thus have some Only-Child tendencies. Lastborns who are *many* years younger than their older siblings are quick to laugh that they were "a mistake" by their parents, but in saying this they often (ironically) shine with Only-Child confidence! They never had to share sibling-style attention, so everyone in the family doted on them.

The Goal

You probably know what to expect by now: Lastborns are most compatible with other Lastborns and with Middle-Children. Lastborns whose next-oldest siblings were 5 or more years older are Virtual Firstborns (the same rule that applies to Middle-Children), so they are also compatible with Firstborns and Only-Children: Refer back to Bob and LaVerne (Profile Edu-5) in the Education chapter to read about a Lastborn (a whopping 15-year difference between him and his next-oldest sibling) and an Only-Child, respectively.

True Lastborns are accustomed to getting their way and getting attention by being cute, and this can be a sore spot when communicating with a true Firstborn or Only-Child. I had a boss who was a Lastborn, and even though she was in her late 50s, she would sometimes talk baby-talk. A Firstborn on our team once confided to me how much that annoyed her, and I explained that our boss' status as a Lastborn helps to explain this behavior. My coworker didn't seem convinced, but it's difficult to explain to a twentysomething why her fiftysomething manager is speaking like a 4-year-old at work.

That's not to say that all Lastborns talk baby-talk, of course! But all Lastborns have retained certain strategies they learned while they were young, from their days of being the family superlative of Cutest, and those strategies come out in adulthood as well—as do the strategies of all the other Birth Order types.

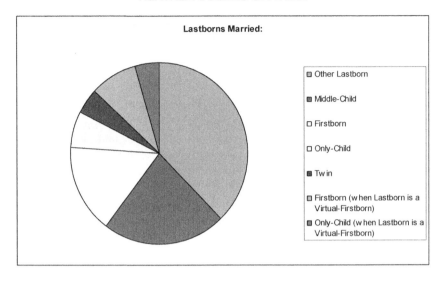

Figure Env-Birth-4: Matrix Study Results of Lastborns' Tendencies in Marriage

Profile Env-Birth-7: Kevin and Kara

These two went to high school and college together, but there were no romantic feelings until they danced with each other at a mutual friend's wedding reception. Then, Kara said, something just "clicked." Here is their Matrix:

	Kevin	Kara	Matrix Points:
Religion (importance: 1–4)	Jewish (4)	Christian—Protestant (3)	–
Education	Bachelor's degree	Bachelor's degree	♥
Spending (1–4)	2	3	♥
Politics (1–4)	2	3	♥
Environment:			
■ Birth Order	Lastborn of four (4 years younger than his next-oldest sibling)	Lastborn of three (1 year younger than her next-oldest sibling)	♥
■ Clean (1–4)	3	3	♥
Chemistry	Type A	Type A	♥
Togetherness	Watching movies, reading, board games, talking		♥
Matrix Score:			7

Something that their Matrix doesn't show is even more dramatic. Kara and Kevin both lost their fathers before they graduated from high school: Kevin's father died when Kevin was only 2, and Kara's father passed away when she was 16. Because they both have the A blood type and are correspondingly empathetic, feelings-oriented people, they can relate to each other's experiences at a very deep level—and sharing the life-changing experience of losing their fathers has strengthened their bond. It makes for a very strong Togetherness factor.

In addition to that, everything else jibes between these two. They have the same Chemistry, Environment (both Birth Order and Cleanliness), and Education-level factors. They both rate themselves as moderates in Spending and Politics; and the Religion factor, though notably different, doesn't appear to be consequential enough to them to create a chasm. Note that their favorite activities to do together aren't intense-action–oriented activities, but rather calm activities that promote closeness—which isn't surprising since they both have the A blood type. (We'll discuss that later in the Chemistry chapter.)

Profile Env-Birth-8: Vernon and Bobbi

Both members of the graduating class of 1940 at the University of Michigan, Bobbi and Vernon are Lastborns who were lucky enough to find each other in the beginning of their adult lives. After more than 60 years of marriage, their Matrix speaks for itself:

	Vernon	Bobbi	Matrix Points:
Religion (importance: 1–4)	Christian—Presbyterian (1)	Christian—Presbyterian (1)	♥
Education	Bachelor's degree	Bachelor's degree	♥
Spending (1–4)	2	4	–
Politics (1–4)	1	1	♥
Environment:			
▪ Birth Order	Lastborn of three (4 years younger than his next-oldest sibling)	Lastborn of four (2 years younger than her next-oldest sibling)	♥
▪ Clean (1–4)	2	2	♥
Chemistry	Type O	Type O	♥
Togetherness	Playing bridge, traveling, reading, golf		♥
Matrix Score:			7

This couple share a Perfect Matrix score of 7, with their only disparate factor being in Spending—yet even there, his moderate stance means they're not on completely opposite ends of the spectrum. They both come from fairly big families and have obvious commonalities across their Matrix…and it doesn't hurt that they naturally root for the same college team: "Go Blue!"

Twins and Compatibility

Classic traits:
- Agreeable and flexible
- Get along well with all types of people—not quick to anger
- Not always very assertive when necessary

People who have a Twin tend to be accustomed to sharing attention and therefore do very well socially with groups. All of the people in this study who were "one-of-Twins" seemed to be, temperamentally, as flexible as Middle-Children (regarding Birth Order compatibility), possibly because they have a less-defined role in the family dynamic than do Firstborns, Lastborns, and Only-Children. They had to figure out how to define themselves individually rather than let others do the defining, as is what happens so clearly with Firstborns and Lastborns.

The Goal

The seven participants who each had a Twin didn't appear to have a clear preference regarding Birth Order, but they did tend toward the extremes: Two were married to Firstborns, one was married to an Only-Child, and the other four were married to Lastborns. None were married to Middle-Children. So it might follow that a Twin prefers someone who has a very clearly defined familial role—whether it be the "leader" or the "baby." After all, they themselves grew up with a somewhat undefined or ambiguous role. This is perhaps one of those areas in which a shared experience isn't necessarily ideal in marriage.

Profile Env-Birth-9: Ken and Gail

Ken is a Twin and is the fourth of six children, and Gail is a Firstborn of three. Twins like Ken do seem to prefer Firstborns and Lastborns, so Gail is an excellent match. They have an Ideal score of 8, as you can see in their Matrix:

82

	Ken	Gail	Matrix Points:
Religion (importance: 1–4)	Christian— Presbyterian (2)	Christian— Presbyterian (2)	♥
Education	Some college	Bachelor's degree	♥
Spending (1–4)	3	2	♥
Politics (1–4)	2	2	♥
Environment:			
▪ Birth Order	Fourth of six (one of Twins)	Firstborn of three	♥
▪ Clean (1–4)	2	2	♥
Chemistry	Type O	Type B	♥
Togetherness	Reading, watching TV, attending their daughters' activities		♥
Matrix Score:			8

They have no major deviations from each other in any of the imperative RESPECT areas—and after more than 25 years of marriage, their formula has proved its viability. Bravo!

Final Thoughts on Birth Order…

One of the first insights we learn when we're very young is where exactly our "place" is in the family, and it largely has to do with our age as compared to everyone else in the family. Children are naïve, but they're not stupid—and at a very young age, we assume roles and devise strategies for ensuring that we are noticed, respected, and even admired as much as possible for our place in the family unit. Therefore, there are certain tendencies among people who shared the same or similar roles while growing up, and we can relate better to others if we're aware of these resulting differences in perspective.

In marriage, a Firstborn will occasionally go into semi-bullying mode just out of a bad old habit; if that Firstborn is married to another Firstborn, they'll understand and even identify with that mode—it might still turn into an argument, but they'll be speaking the same bully language and they'll get over it. Similarly, Middle-Children expect people to figure out how to get along with each other; it comes naturally to them, because they learned their own strategies for peacemaking at a very young age. Lastborns are adept at being and acting cute, and they get by at all stages of life by charming those around them with their adorableness. Only-Children like to be leaders because they're comfortable, based on experience, being the one everyone focuses on, the one everyone admires and gives responsibility to—even the one everyone expects to "get along on their own" just fine. A Twin tends to particularly admire someone who is "their own person," and others are attracted to a Twin because of their adaptability.

If you're aware of these tendencies, you'll know what to look for and what to steer clear from in finding your ideal match. Everyone is different, so pay attention to someone's assumed role in relationships, even in conversations, and their associated communication patterns when talking in a group.

All this said, there are some overlapping traits between Birth Order and Chemistry, as delineated in the next chapter! But first, we must explore the second part of Environment.

~ Cheat Sheet ~	
RESPECT	**Answer: People who are... Should look for...**
Environment Part 1: Birth order/role in the family	**Only-Children...** other Only-Children, Firstborns, or Virtual Firstborns (not Middle-Children or true Lastborns) **Firstborns...** other Firstborns, Only-Children, Virtual Firstborns, or Middle-Children (not true Lastborns) **Middle-Children...** other Middle-Children, Firstborns, or Lastborns (not Only-Children or Twins) **Lastborns...** other Lastborns or Middle-Children (not Only-Children or Firstborns) **Twins...** anyone except Middle-Children

Part 2: *Surroundings* Environment (Cleanliness)

Why This Is Important

Happy couples tend to develop certain habits of cleaning parts of the house, doing laundry, and expectations (whether high or low) of Cleanliness, and that's why this factor is so important. It's a cliché that men throw their dirty socks and underwear on the floor; it's also a cliché that women hang their undergarments over the shower door. But these aren't universal habits by any means, and men who *don't* throw their dirty laundry on the floor should marry women who *don't* hang their undergarments over the shower.

Don't rationalize that you, if you're a clean freak, will somehow "convert" the other person into a tidy person as well, or even that you'll ensure that the other person doesn't live like a bum (if that's how they now live). If you're the *opposite* of a clean freak, don't rationalize that you'll make the other person more mellow—you won't.

The Goal

Who you're most compatible with: *In Cleanliness, it's best to be the same number or only one "notch" away from the other person on the 1–4 Cleanliness scale.*

You'll want Mr/s. Right to be the same number as you, or only one notch away from you, on the 1–4 Environment (Cleanliness) scale. For the survey, the numbers were arbitrarily chosen as "1" being Very Tidy and "4" being Not Very Tidy—please note that the 1 and the 4 don't presume one is better than the other. Your personal preference is what matters.

When dating, it's best to observe the living area of the other person. Are they about as neat as you are? If not, bring it up lightly: If they're a clean-freak, say something observant like "You really keep everything immaculate!" or, if they're not-so-tidy, smile and say, "This place looks very cozy and lived-in!" You might find out that the observed tidiness, or lack thereof, is actually due to their roommate or a cleaning service. Either way, you'll find out the other person's expectation level or tolerance level in the area of Cleanliness.

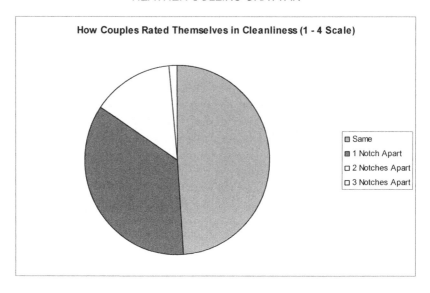

Figure Env-Clean-1: Matrix Study Results of Cleanliness Tendencies in Marriage

Ultra-Clean

Although men are the target of ribbing for their lack of Cleanliness, the survey's results show that this isn't the case at all. Men who rated themselves as a 1 on this scale rarely married women who weren't either a 1 or 2—in fact, only six of the 233 couples who answered this question ranked the man as a 1 and the woman as a 3, and *none* of these 1-rating men were married to a woman who rated themselves as a 4.

However, on the converse, 20 women who rated themselves as a 1 on this scale married men who rated as a 3, and three 1-rating women married men who pinned themselves as a 4. Thus, women generally displayed more tolerance and adaptability in this area than men did— probably because fastidious men tend to assume that women "should be" very tidy, whereas women don't assume that about men.

Profile Env-Clean-1: Wes and Susan

Sharing a penchant for tidiness, Susan and Wes appreciate immaculate surroundings—as is evidenced in their Matrix:

	Wes	Susan	Matrix Points:
Religion (importance: 1–4)	Christian— Episcopalian (2)	Christian— Episcopalian (2)	♥
Education	Bachelor's degree	Bachelor's degree	♥
Spending (1–4)	3	2	♥
Politics (1–4)	2	2	♥
Environment:			
▪ **Birth Order**	Only-Child	Firstborn of two	♥
▪ **Clean (1–4)**	1	1	♥
Chemistry	Type B	Type O	♥
Togetherness	Boating, walking, designing homes, golf, hiking		♥
Matrix Score:			8

After more than 40 years of marriage, this couple have developed an enriching life together based on a foundation of common values and experiences. They're both observant Episcopalians, moderately conservative, and moderately frugal; these Firstborns (Wes is a "super-Firstborn" as an Only-Child) also have bachelor's degrees, compatible blood types, and plenty of Togetherness activities.

Profile Env-Clean-2: Tom and Nicki

For this question, Nicki circled the "1" and put three asterisks next to it—she's a total clean freak! So it's very good that she married a man who's on the same side of this equation: Tom ranked himself as a 2. Here is their Matrix:

	Tom	Nicki	Matrix Points:
Religion (importance: 1–4)	Christian— Catholic (1)	Christian— Presbyterian (1)	♥
Education	Bachelor's degree	Master's degree	♥
Spending (1–4)	2	4	–
Politics (1–4)	1	2	♥
Environment:			
▪ Birth Order	Second of three (4 years younger than his older sibling)	Third of four (1 year younger than her next-oldest sibling)	♥
▪ Clean (1–4)	2	1	♥
Chemistry	Type O	Type B	♥
Togetherness	Listening to music, taking care of their child, walking, laughing		♥
Matrix Score:			7

Nicki and Tom added on the back of their survey two other points of interest that happen to fit perfectly here in the Environment chapter: "(1) We both have sisters who became pregnant in high school and kept their babies. Both of these babies, our oldest nephews (ages 24 and 21), are very special to us and our families. (2) We are both very much parent and family pleasers."

That second point is a shining example of the peacemaking behaviors that are typical of Middle-Children like Nicki and Tom—making them an excellent two-for-one profile here in the Environment chapter!

They have a Perfect score of 7: Both are well Educated, on the conservative side Politically, and have strong Chemistry. They might have occasional spats over finances, given their two-notch difference in Spending; but they were effusive in their list of Togetherness activities— Nicki actually wrote, "…Laughing (stupid stuff)," which demonstrates a common wavelength they share and an ease in their communication together. They click.

Tidy

Profile Env-Clean-3: Ren and Tammy

This couple are a prime example of the *mode* for this question (i.e., the most frequently occurring answer), with both spouses rating themselves as a 2. In fact, 61 of the 233 couples who answered this question consider themselves to be 2&2. Incidentally, the second-most-frequent combination was 1&2 (like Tom and Nicki in the previous profile), with 51 couples describing themselves that way.

Tammy and Ren have been married for more than 20 years, and they have an Ideal score of 8 on their Matrix:

	Ren	Tammy	Matrix Points:
Religion (importance: 1–4)	Christian— Presbyterian (1)	Christian— Presbyterian (1)	♥
Education	Bachelor's degree	Bachelor's degree	♥
Spending (1–4)	2	2	♥
Politics (1–4)	2	2	♥
Environment:			
▪ **Birth Order**	Firstborn of four	Second of three (4½ years younger than her older sibling)	♥
▪ **Clean (1–4)**	2	2	♥
Chemistry	Type A	Type A	♥
Togetherness	Church activities, reading, walking/exercising, going out		♥
Matrix Score:			8

Tammy is 4½ years younger than her older sibling, and this renders her as a Virtual Firstborn—corresponding nicely to Ren's Firstborn status. Everything else matches ideally.

Profile Env-Clean-4: Doug and Sue

When you live near the Atlantic Ocean and enjoy spending weekends out on your boat, you can't really be too much of a stickler for Cleanliness. Saltwater can make things feel sticky, and some water will undoubtedly find its way inside the boat after snorkeling and fishing. So the Environment can get a bit messy during this glamorous pastime.

Sue and Doug have been married for more than 30 years, and they enjoy boating together regularly. They rate themselves on either side of the Cleanliness scale, though only one notch apart:

	Doug	Sue	Matrix Points:
Religion (importance: 1–4)	Christian— Methodist (3)	Christian— Catholic (3)	♥
Education	Bachelor's degree	Some college	♥
Spending (1–4)	2	2	♥
Politics (1–4)	3	3	♥
Environment:			
▪ **Birth Order**	Firstborn of two	Lastborn of four (3 years younger than her next-oldest sibling)	♥
▪ **Clean (1–4)**	3	2	♥
Chemistry	Type A	Type A	♥
Togetherness	Boating, traveling, scuba diving		♥
Matrix Score:			8

They match extremely well across the board. Their only potential weak spot is their Birth Order, where there might be slight differences in confidence levels or related social behaviors; other than that, they both attended college, are fairly frugal, are moderately observant Christians, and share the same Chemistry. They can celebrate their Ideal score of 8 with a toast of bubbly on the Atlantic. Cheers!

Final Thoughts on Cleanliness…

Just like all the other basic values we're talking about throughout this book, you do, personally, have a set of assumptions when it comes to Cleanliness. You're either more toward the side of picking up messes and keeping things neat, or you're more toward the side of allowing messes here and there because it's not that big of a deal to you. Either way, it's best to be fairly similar to each other in this very basic assumption and in your related cleaning habits. Otherwise, resentment may build up over time. A very fastidious person will be constantly picking up the messes left by the other one. Let's not let that happen!

Incidentally, one thing that wasn't included in the Matrix survey but has been consistently observed is that pack-rats tend to marry purgers. (Opposites!) In other words, folks who tend to keep everything tend to marry folks who tend to go on throwaway sprees. As long as both spouses understand the parameters of what sorts of things can be saved (and where) and what things can be discarded, this works out just fine. These opposite characteristics actually complement each other, as the saver tends to keep things that the purger would actually want to save, and the purger naturally pressures the saver to throw away things that may unnecessarily waste precious space.

For example, this is particularly helpful when the saver has kept leftovers for too long, and the purger has been given the green light to "be the one" to throw away those old leftovers—because the purger will happily oblige. But this status as a saver or purger is something that can't usually be determined *before* marriage—just rest assured that it's a natural and healthy combination.

Final Thoughts on Environment (Birth Order and Cleanliness)…

Experts have differing opinions about Birth Order tendencies as far as compatibility is concerned, but suffice it to say that if you grow up thinking of yourself in a certain "place" in the family (and we all do), it follows that you will naturally be on the same or similar wavelength as someone who shares your perspective. You'll tend to react to things similarly—such as whether or not to get involved in an issue or problem that others are experiencing, or whether or not a leader is making decisions you agree with. You'll also react similarly as far as whether you naturally take charge of things, whether you go into cutie-pie mode, or whether you go into peacemaking/collaborating mode.

And as far as Cleanliness is concerned, just take a quick look-see around the house or apartment of the person you're dating. You'll get a pretty good idea as to whether or not this person lives too differently than the way you want to. That said, if the person is still living with their parents and the house is either too immaculate or too messy for your taste, then look at the person's room. Your companion may differ from their parents in this regard.

Don't stop yourself from analyzing a person's Environment, especially if you're starting to get serious in the dating relationship. These are core qualities about a person.

~ Cheat Sheet ~	
RESPECT	**Answer: People who are... Should look for...**
Environment Part 1: Birth order/ role in the family	**Only-Children...** other Only-Children, Firstborns, or Virtual Firstborns (not Middle-Children or true Lastborns) **Firstborns...** other Firstborns, Only-Children, Virtual Firstborns, or Middle-Children (not true Lastborns) **Middle-Children...** other Middle-Children, First-borns, or Lastborns (not Only-Children or Twins) **Lastborns...** other Lastborns or Middle-Children (not Only-Children or Firstborns) **Twins...** anyone except Middle-Children
Environment Part 2: Neat/clean (1–4)	...Look for someone who ranks themselves as the same or only one "notch" away from you

RESPECT

Chapter 8: Chemistry

What is your blood type?	O A B AB

"Sexual attraction pairs people, but does not match them."
— *Mason Cooley*

Sometimes researchers discover something totally unexpected during the course of their study—and this was the case when Joseph Christiano (who graciously wrote the Foreword to this book) and Dr. Steven M. Weissberg studied a large group of people for the purpose of analyzing their exercise patterns and other physical commonalities as they might pertain to one's blood type. As documented in their diet/exercise book *The Answer Is In Your Bloodtype*, they did, as they expected, find many similar characteristics.

But they also noticed an unexpected pattern among the married participants in their study. (Get ready to throw away those horoscopes in your drawer!)

First, it stood out that there were a number of couples participating in their analysis who shared the rare AB blood type. This piqued their interest, and they noticed that a disproportionately high number of married people in their study had the same blood type as each other. Christiano and Weissberg also noted that, other than these same-type couples, matchups of O&B and A&AB types appeared in higher numbers than the others.[1]

In the U.S., Type O comprises about 48% of the population, Type A about 37%, Type B about 11%, and Type AB about 4%.[5] (Interestingly, black Americans have shown slightly different statistics when analyzed as an isolated group: Types O and AB had almost identical statistics as the overall population, but Type A represented only about 27% [about 10% less than overall] and Type B about 20% [almost 10% more].)[6]

Indeed, in the 1920s, Japanese psychology professor Takeji Furukawa observed that people of the same blood type—O, A, B, or AB—

had consistently similar personality traits, on a very basic level.[3] Later, the father-son team of Masahiko Nomi and Noshitaka Nomi further refined blood-type psychology.[4] In the 1990s, author Dr. Peter D'Adamo's book *Eat Right 4 Your Type* describes the phenomenon of how people with the same blood type tend to metabolize various foods in the same way—and in often opposing ways than people of other blood types—and he also echoes the observation that people with the same blood type tend to share certain personality tendencies when compared to those with different blood types.[3]

Sure enough, in compiling the data for this book from the Matrix survey, participants' responses largely jibed with Christiano and Weissberg's findings. People indeed tended to marry people with the same blood type as each other, and outside of that parameter were O&B and A&AB couples, and a statistics-defying relative *lack* of O&A couples—of which there should have been a larger percentage if this were a nonissue.

Considering all this, I've concluded that God has allowed us to discover part of His blueprint on how our personalities are wired, in regards to blood type. We already knew about the importance of the biological component (such as in organ donation), so we really shouldn't be surprised that there are accompanying sociological tendencies that remain from when the given blood type entered the scene of the world. (Japan is way ahead of the West in regards to understanding the blood type–personality connection, by the way.)

Why This Is Important

Chemistry can be felt. You know when you feel Chemistry with someone. You can't define it, and it doesn't necessarily have to do with how good-looking or smart the other person is. There's just a strong attraction, and you can't get rid of it. It might even make you lovesick.

That's why Chemistry—biochemistry, to be precise—is one of the most important factors in compatibility (but not the *only* important factor). If you don't feel physically attracted to the other person, someday this person will probably make you feel sick, bored, and stuck in a relationship that isn't fun anymore.

If you get nothing else from this chapter, please remember that feeling physically attracted to the other person is extremely important in compatibility. Don't talk yourself into feeling attracted to another person just because you "should." The innate attraction may be felt right away or grow gradually, but it's either there or it isn't.

...And Why It Makes Sense

God has designed each of us in a special, thorough, individual way, and yet there are observable patterns among us. We each feel naturally attracted to certain people (whether as friends or as romantic interests) and have almost nothing to say to certain other people, even if we do have commonalities such as belonging to the same organization. We may be doing the same activity—like eating lunch—with different people, yet with one person we may feel like lunch isn't long enough to discuss everything we want to talk about, but the conversation (if any) goes painfully and awkwardly slow with another.

This doesn't happen coincidentally or randomly.

Your blood type is an integral part of the great design of your own biochemical makeup, and it follows that your sociobiology affects the way you think and behave. This theory is not at all akin to astrology or the like, because it has nothing to do with coincidence and everything to do with our physical makeup—you are *you*, right down to the cellular level. And yes, this has nothing to do with a person's beliefs and everything else, which is why this is only one-eighth of the RESPECT compatibility factors.

It is generally agreed-upon by researchers that the Type O "hunters" were the first humans; with the agrarian society, the farmers' body chemistry adapted to be Type A "gatherers"; as people moved to cold climates and started domesticating animals (and drank their milk) came the biochemistry adjustment of Type B "nomads"; and when As started blending with Bs, Type AB appeared on the world stage.

Somewhat like a computer's operating system, blood type refers to how we're programmed, or wired. In the Matrix survey, some combinations were clearly noted to work well together, and others not generally quite as well.

The Goal

Who you're most compatible with: *People of each blood type (O, A, B, and AB) tend to be more attracted to, and get along better with, those of the same type as themselves; they are also highly compatible with one of the other three blood types: Types A and AB are very compatible with each other, and Types O and B are very compatible with each other.*

If you find yourself falling in love with someone outside of these parameters—let's say you have the A blood type but your new love is Type O—be sure to analyze whether you have the other RESPE_T factors in common (including both Environment factors), and consider whether you truly feel romantically drawn to the other person or whether you're rather like best friends. If that strong romantic feeling does exist, there shouldn't be a problem.

"Baloney! I'm not buying it…"

Not convinced? I wouldn't be, either. Claims like this demand plenty of supporting data to back them up.

If the blood-type connection were bogus, there should have been maybe one—two at the most by sheer coincidence—participating couples in this study in which both partners were the rare AB blood type. After all, only about 4% of Americans (most participants in the Matrix study are Americans) have the AB type. Yet, an amazingly high number of six couples in this survey who answered this question are both of the AB blood type. That's a binomial probability factor of .0016, or a chance of about 4 in 1,000,000! So, either I should be playing the lottery, or the theory of the blood-type/personality connection has some merit.

Following are the four blood types, the general personality tendencies of those who have each type, and some observations regarding how these tendencies are important in relationships. (I've even included an appropriate Beatitude for each, because it fit so well with Type A—you'll see why—so everyone gets one.)

Type O

General tendencies:
- Socially oriented, lots of friends/acquaintances
- Perceptive about people's motives and modus operandi
- Easily give in to peer pressure
- Tend to be materialistic
- Having fun is very important
- "Depth" not a concern when making friends
- Aggressive tendencies when out of balance
- Work better on teams than the other three types
- Natural carnivores
- Superlative: Most Fun
- Beatitude: "Blessed are the merciful"

I have to first beg the Type O reader not to think, "Well, that describes *everyone!*" That's just not true! Compare your qualities with those of the other types as listed in this chapter, and you'll notice the distinct differences.

Most Type Os I know quickly dismiss the notion that blood type has anything to do with anything that isn't medically related. They tend to think that "everyone" has this blood type, so how could it matter? Such generalizing is part of their nature—author Peter Constantine even dubbed Type Os as "generalists." (Contrast with Type Bs, whom Constantine calls "specialists.")[4]

Generally speaking, Type Os are the most social, the most active, and live the longest of all four blood groups. They *get energy* from being with lots of people in social settings—they don't necessarily have to get to know the people, just do a little chatting, maybe a little drinking, or play a pickup game of basketball or bridge. They can dialogue in just about any subject, because they like knowing a little about everything around them. Contrast this with Type As, who usually *feel drained* and need some "alone time" after a lot of social interaction, such as after a large party. Type Os are the ones who are the first to be invited to parties and concerts, even by those who are only acquaintances.

I gave the "merciful" beatitude to Type Os because of their general ability to forgive and forget more readily than the other three types—and to tolerate others' idiosyncrasies without a lot of overanalyzing like the other three types tend to do. While a Type A, B, or AB may still feel hurt by another's words or actions, a Type O is more likely to mercifully get past it, and just strike up a conversation about something else. Perhaps this is because the Type O can see the big picture of the person—their strengths and their weaknesses, as part of the whole person—rather than getting "stuck in the weeds" like the rest of us are wont to do…!

Although this ability to ignore negative idiosyncrasies of others is usually a wonderful trait, especially in regular friendship- or coworker-type relationships, it sometimes means that deeply felt feelings go unexpressed and the relationship retains a shallowness. If this happens in a marriage, Peter Constantine calls it an "empty-shell marriage."[4] But because Type Os can enjoy talking about superficial matters, they don't tend to make judgments about others as often as the other three types do. Even if they do judge someone, the other person can easily redeem themselves by proving to be a friend after all. The other three types are less forgiving, or take longer to forgive and forget.

Type Os love to talk about events, and they enjoy telling jokes or funny stories—the "fun" aspect is important to them. Contrast this with Type As, who most enjoy in-depth discussions about concepts, feelings, and thoughts; and with Type Bs, who are happiest with people with whom they can freely discuss a balance of the fun and superficial (such as a sports game) and the serious and thought-provoking (such as the coach's personal issues) without any transition or apparent provocation.

The Goal

In terms of compatibility, Type Os prove to have the happiest and most stable marriages when paired with other Os or with Type Bs. (Less so with Type As or ABs.) The Type B's bent toward discussing things and events meshes well with the Type O, and they can also enjoy discussing deep feelings and concepts. Type Os do enjoy variety, and a Type B usually offers plenty of variety because of their own need for balance, their oddball traits, and their general lack of social fears.

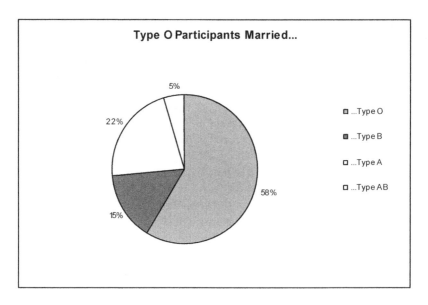

Figure C-1: Matrix Study Results of Type O Tendencies in Marriage

Looking at the above pie chart, Type Os married a significantly higher percentage of other Type Os than the aforementioned 48% population figure. They also married a higher percentage of Type Bs than the 11% population figure—and a much lower percentage of Type As than the 37% population figure. But just to reiterate, this isn't necessarily a game-changer. There are seven other RESPE_T areas.

Highly Compatible Marriage Combination: Type O and Type O

Profile C-1: Mike and Meg

This young couple possesses all the qualities pointing toward a long-lasting marriage. Both sociable Type Os, they earn an Ideal score of 8:

	Mike	Meg	Matrix Points:
Religion (importance: 1–4)	Christian (1)	Christian (1)	♥
Education	Bachelor's degree	Master's degree	♥
Spending (1–4)	2	2	♥
Politics (1–4)	1	2	♥
Environment:			
▪ Birth Order	Firstborn of two	Fifth of six (2 years younger than her next-oldest sibling)	♥
▪ Clean (1–4)	1	2	♥
Chemistry	Type O	Type O	♥
Togetherness	Playing with our children, dinner with others and by ourselves		♥
Matrix Score:			8

The activities they list in their Togetherness answer are active and people-oriented endeavors, which are classic characteristics of their blood-type Chemistry. Conversely, Type A participants tended to list more passive, introverted pastimes than did Type Os.

Also note that Meg's Middle-Child status ensures her compatibility with anyone who has siblings, and Mike's status as Firstborn of two fills the bill just fine. Both are devout Christians, are on the conservative side of the Political scale, are highly educated, and are fairly tidy and frugal. If other young people follow their lead, we'll halt the current trend of "starter marriages"!

Highly Compatible Marriage Combination: Type O and Type B

Profile C-2: Julian and Kim

Demonstrating Type Os' interestingly strong attraction to Type Bs is this thirtysomething couple: Kim and Julian first met at their company's Christmas party, where they kissed. Quite a bit of time passed before they even really spoke to each other again—and eventually, they started dating. They quickly came to realize their all-around compatibility beyond the strong Chemistry that brought them together in the first place. Here is their Matrix:

	Julian	Kim	Matrix Points:
Religion (importance: 1–4)	Christian— Presbyterian (1)	Christian— Presbyterian (1)	♥
Education	Master's degree	Some college	–
Spending (1–4)	3	3	♥
Politics (1–4)	1	1	♥
Environment:			
▪ Birth Order	Third of three (4 years younger than his next-oldest sibling)	Firstborn of three	♥
▪ Clean (1–4)	2	1	♥
Chemistry	Type O	Type B	♥
Togetherness	Walking at the park and at the beach, volleyball, reading, dinner out		♥
Matrix Score:			7

Kim was raised Baptist, so it wasn't too much of a change to switch to another Protestant denomination. (In fact, Kim told me that they've since moved, and they now attend a Baptist church!) They are both very Religious, very conservative Politically, fastidious, and relatively unfrugal. They each come from a family of five, and both went to college.

When you're suddenly attracted to someone who turns out to have all the right qualities for you, that deep-seated attraction can last "till death do us part." Kim and Julian have all the ingredients necessary for a lifelong journey of joy and happiness together.

Caveat Compatibility Trend: Type O and Type AB + Firstborn and Non-Firstborn Combination

Although Types O and AB didn't have noticeable compatibility with each other in Weissberg and Christiano's study,[1] the Matrix survey showed a unique trend in this area, and it bucks the Birth Order trend as well: In *every* couple with the O&AB combination, one of the two in the couple was a Firstborn, and the spouse was a non-Firstborn (i.e., anything but a Firstborn). Further, in most of them, the Type O was the Firstborn and was the husband, and (obviously) the Type AB was the non-Firstborn and was the wife.

100

Profile C-3: Michael and Susan

Michael grew up in the ghetto and his parents divorced, but his drive for success (very characteristic of Type O) gave him the wherewithal to earn a master's degree. His status as a Firstborn lent itself to self-confidence, which surely helped give him a mental boost to overcome those obstacles (ghetto and parents' divorce).

But unlike his parents, he's happily married—to Susan. Susan has an enthusiastic personality as a well-balanced Type AB, and her upbringing as a Middle-Child renders her highly compatible with anyone except an Only-Child or a Twin.

They thus satisfy the stringently compatible combination of Type O married to a Type AB with one of them being a Firstborn and the other being a non-Firstborn, so they indeed get a point in the Chemistry factor:

	Michael	Susan	Matrix Points:
Religion (importance: 1–4)	Open (1)	Christian—Catholic (4)	♥
Education	Master's degree	Some college	–
Spending (1–4)	4	3	♥
Politics (1–4)	4	4	♥
Environment:			
▪ Birth Order	Firstborn of 13	Sixth of nine	♥
▪ Clean (1–4)	2	1	♥
Chemistry	Type O	Type AB	♥
Togetherness	Walking at the park and at the beach, volleyball, reading, dinner out		♥
Matrix Score:			7

In their Matrix, you can easily see all the things they enjoy doing together as well as their many shared values. They both consider themselves very liberal Politically, and his answer of "Open" to the Religion question does jibe with her lack of enthusiasm for her Catholic background. Also note that they both come from very large families, so they're both accustomed to sharing the attention. I'm sure they'll enjoy each other for the rest of their lives.

Type A

General tendencies:
- Feelings-oriented
- Most intuitive of the four types
- Peacemakers—reconciliation is more important to them than justice
- Enjoy one-on-one conversation much more than group-talk
- Self-deprecating, understanding, great listeners
- Paranoid tendencies when out of balance
- Tend to stick to rules too inflexibly; germophobes; close to the vest
- Naturally drawn to parenting and teaching
- Natural herbivores
- Superlative: Most Well-Liked
- Beatitude: "Blessed are the peacemakers"

Type As are everyone's best friends. When I'm talking with a Type A who is being self-condescending, sometimes I can't stop myself from blurting out this beatitude—they truly don't give themselves credit for being such good people. And I can't help but point out how wonderfully humble they are. Their superlative is likely to embarrass them, even though it would be easy to prove by an anonymous survey of the people in the groups in which they are involved (school, work, church, club, etc.).

Type As often have a very calming effect on their friends, and they love to have conversations discussing theories, feelings, or relationships. Contrast this with Type Os, who usually prefer discussing social events, sports/games, and telling jokes and stories—though because Type Os are generalists, they can happily discuss feelings as well! They just won't be as engrossed in the topic as the Type A will be. Thus, the Type A needs to be careful not to take it personally if a Type O seems to want to move along in the conversation after a while—the Type O is "over it" and doesn't want to talk about the topic anymore or get too deep, while the Type A still has feelings to mull over and wants to delve deeper. In an A&O marriage, this can be a recurring problem. Interestingly, four of the five couples who filed for divorce within a year after filling out this survey were A&O couples.

Type A prefers one-on-one bonding—again, contrast with the Type O's tendency to have lots of friends, and several "best" friends (not just one). Type As are usually excellent listeners, too. Oh yeah—and they have the best hair (though they're self-deprecating, so they're not likely to agree!), so Type ABs who favor their A side in regards to their hair are duly lucky. Yes, I'm jealous.

The Goal

In regards to compatibility, Type As tend to do best with other As or with ABs. (Less so with Type Os or Bs.) Type As highly value avoiding heated arguments; they're often willing to relent in order to reestablish peace, rather than stand on principle and possibly cause lasting friction. This is one thing that makes them somewhat less compatible with Type Bs, because Bs usually don't mind having discussions that might become a bit heated—Bs consider such dialogue a means to reach common logical understanding or to hash out ideas. Of the four types, Type As are the least likely to agree with governmental policies favoring entering into war.

The upside to their peacemaking gifts is that they're so agreeable! But they don't always defend their own interests. One of the divorced couples in this study were both Type As: Their families pressured them to get married to each other, and their natural tendency toward peacemaking pushed them to go ahead with the wedding.

People who are extremely quiet and to-themselves until someone brings them out of their shell—then suddenly, they become overly chatty and clingy to that person—are usually Type As! If this type of person can find another who shares this quality, an excellent marriage can result if they're clingy with each other.

Incidentally, if a Type A doesn't demonstrate much humbleness, they're out of balance and would do well to make some mild lifestyle adjustments, and possibly get therapy, because their paranoid tendencies can ultimately be hurtful to others and to themselves. This can range from self-exile from society to overblown fits of rage. (Interestingly, O.J. and Nicole Brown Simpson were both Type As, which explains why they were attracted to each other in the first place despite their disparate backgrounds. One wonders if maybe their Chemistry overrode good judgment.)

U.S. President Richard Nixon, who was a Type A, has this as his tombstone's epitaph: "The greatest honor history can bestow is the title of peacemaker." Although Nixon is most famous for the Watergate scandal of 1974, one of his greatest accomplishments was striking up a friendship between the U.S. and China. Obviously, he'd rather be remembered for his peacemaking qualities and achievements, which is where he excelled—and is right in line with his natural sociological and psychological Chemistry.

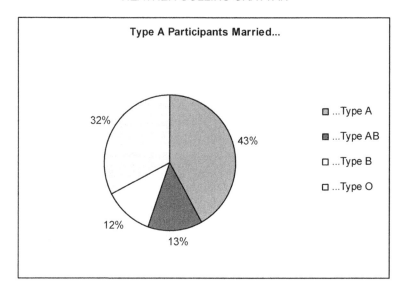

Type A Participants Married...

32%
43%
12%
13%

□ ...Type A
■ ...Type AB
□ ...Type B
□ ...Type O

Figure C-2: Matrix Study Results of Type A Tendencies in Marriage

Notice in this figure that Type As showed a higher percentage of attraction toward other Type As: greater than that 37% general population figure. Likewise, they're attracted to Type ABs, which are only 4% of the population but represent a surprising 13% here. Type Os are a relatively low 32% as compared to their 48% general-population figure.

Highly Compatible Marriage Combination: Type A and Type A

Profile C-4: David and Virginia

After more than 50 years of marriage, Virginia and David's union has withstood the myriad trials and issues that unavoidably pop up in everyday life—which, in their case, included World War II. These two Type As first dated by going to church together, and they still attend that same church every Sunday. Here is their Matrix:

	David	Virginia	Matrix Points:
Religion (importance: 1–4)	Christian—Presbyterian (1)	Christian—Presbyterian (1)	♥
Education	Some college	Bachelor's degree	♥
Spending (1–4)	1	2	♥
Politics (1–4)	1	1	♥
Environment:			
▪ Birth Order	Firstborn of two	Only-Child	♥
▪ Clean (1–4)	1	1	♥
Chemistry	Type A	Type A	♥
Togetherness	Reading, jigsaw puzzles, watching TV, Bible studies, music, trips, friends		♥
Matrix Score:			8

Notice that the Togetherness activities they listed first are relatively passive, cerebral activities—classic of Type As, which you can contrast with the typical answers of our Type O participants, which are usually more active. They're both very Religious, very conservative, very fastidious, and pretty frugal, and both are Firstborns—Virginia is, in fact, a "super-Firstborn" as an Only-Child. With so much in common, no wonder they made it to their Golden Anniversary.

Profile C-5: Peter and Katherine

A textbook-style pairing of two Type As, Katherine and Peter earn an Ideal score of 8. After more than a dozen years of marriage and four adorable kids, this relationship has already withstood through quite a bit. Their young children have had to endure eye surgeries to correct inherited vision deficiencies, and Peter served in Iraq after the 9/11/2001 attacks.

These are examples of the sort of unforeseen circumstances that young lovebirds don't anticipate…and why it's so, so important to have a solid foundation of common values and perspectives before embarking on a lifelong commitment. Here is their Matrix:

	Peter	Katherine	Matrix Points:
Religion (importance: 1–4)	Christian—Presbyterian (2)	Christian—Presbyterian (2)	♥
Education	Master's degree	Bachelor's degree	♥
Spending (1–4)	2	3	♥
Politics (1–4)	2	2	♥
Environment:			
▪ Birth Order	Lastborn of four (3 years younger than his next-oldest sibling)	Lastborn of three (8 years younger than her next-oldest sibling)	♥
▪ Clean (1–4)	3	2	♥
Chemistry	Type A	Type A	♥
Togetherness	Camping, dining, visiting family, attending their children's functions		♥
Matrix Score:			8

Note that they are the same or just one notch apart in *all* aspects. They are both Lastborns (with Katherine as a Virtual Firstborn, but a true Lastborn nevertheless), and they were quite effusive in listing Togetherness activities.

Katherine and Peter were able to lean on each other for constant comfort and encouragement during their children's medical evaluations and operations. They've proven they'll stick together through thick and thin, "in sickness and in health." I can personally report that theirs are some of the happiest kids I've ever seen.

Highly Compatible Marriage Combination: Type A and Type AB

Probably the most intriguing thing about the Type A pie chart (Figure C-2) is the incredibly high compatibility rate with Type ABs: 13%, even though Type ABs comprise only about 4% of the U.S. population. Type As tend to find them all right. If more Type ABs existed, this figure would probably be much greater than 13%.

Profile C-6: Matthew and Ann

A shining example of the rare Type AB being attracted to a Type A, Ann and Matthew are a natural fit:

	Matthew	Ann	Matrix Points:
Religion (importance: 1–4)	Christian— Catholic (1)	Christian— Catholic (1)	♥
Education	Bachelor's degree	Bachelor's degree	♥
Spending (1–4)	3	3	♥
Politics (1–4)	2	2	♥
Environment:			
▪ Birth Order	Lastborn of six (12 years younger than his next-oldest sibling)	Lastborn of three (6 years younger than her next-oldest sibling)	♥
▪ Clean (1–4)	2	2	♥
Chemistry	Type A	Type AB	♥
Togetherness	Swimming, helping our son with homework, relaxing		♥
Matrix Score:			8

They represent the full complement of RESPECT attributes: Both are very religious Catholics (R), have earned their college diplomas (E), are not very frugal (S), are conservative (P), are Lastborns but Virtual Firstborns (E1), are moderately tidy (E2), are compatible Types A and AB (C), and enjoy lots of everyday activities (T), like helping their son with his homework or just relaxing. And after more than a decade of marriage, these two can count on many more days of R&R together.

The Elephant in the Room: Type A and Type O, and Their Compatibility

Because Type As and Type Os together comprise about 85% of the population of the United States, and close to that percentage in the rest of the world as well, they often find each other in marriage simply due to their sheer numbers. And although I've observed that this union isn't always the most comfortable or natural of combinations, this combination can work well as long as neither partner is an extreme example of their blood type—i.e., super-sensitive Type As won't match well in the long run with Type Os, and super-aggressive Type Os won't match well with Type As—because they're simply too different.

Indeed, true to our RESPECT Principle, the A&O couples who were very happy together *were* compatible in the other 7 factors! The couples who weren't so happy, in fact, had notable area(s) in which they were too dissimilar.

If an O and A are going to get married, they should first realize each other's motivators and tendencies. If *either* partner doesn't appreciate the inherent differences about each other, the couple is likely to have communication problems eventually. This combination will work out best if first the Type O develops an understanding of the A's tendency toward: (1) introspective analysis, (2) deeply felt emotions, and (3) aversion to lots of group-oriented activities. Likewise, the Type A should realize that the Type O will never grow out of enjoying group-oriented activities and will strive to be successful and to stand out. (Even relatively introverted or private Type Os still like being where the action is, whether or not they're an active participant in the group.)

Where As and Os do meet is their shared tendency to highly value what others think of them, unlike Bs and ABs. One Type A participant told me he'd heard that people with the A blood type are the "most popular"! While popularity and "coolness" might be attributed more overtly to Type Os, Type As are the most likeable thanks to their high scores in friendliness and humbleness—which are universally attractive and thus "popular" qualities. (If someone tells you how great you are, you'll naturally like that person!) While Type Bs and ABs can easily get angry at people who are trying to get them to do things they don't want to do, typical As and Os will usually go with the flow, or attempt to nonconfrontationally get out of an unappealing activity.

Bottom line: No combination is out of the question, because everyone is different. That said, if this theory held no water, our statistics would have shown a tendency for A&O marriages to be as consistently harmonious as the A&AB and O&B combinations—but that simply isn't the case.

But again, there are plenty of exceptions, and these exceptions demonstrate that you can match in the rest of the RESPE_T factors and still have a perfectly happy marriage. You'll next meet Patrick and Kathleen in Profile C-7, and Walt and Charlotte in Profile C-8. Also see how A&O works in Profile R-1 (Bill and Laura, in the Religion chapter), Profile P-2 (Tom and Ann, in the Politics chapter), and later in Profile L-2 (James and Nadine, in the Lesser Issues in Compatibility chapter).

Profile C-7: Patrick and Kathleen

I would have bet (and lost) money that my co-worker Kathleen was a Type O. I'd based my guess on the fact that she was an enthusiastic player on the company softball team and is very extroverted—highly active and social, which are quintessential Type O characteristics. As it turns out, her Type A father passed away when she was just 22 months old, so she and her siblings were raised by their Type O mother. Kathleen picked up these Type O traits while growing up, and she learned to closely identify with and even mimic her mother's personality traits.

So it's logical that she feels comfortable in marriage with her Type O husband, Patrick, especially since they have a Perfect score of 7. Here is their Matrix:

	Patrick	Kathleen	Matrix Points:
Religion (importance: 1–4)	Christian—Methodist/ Presbyterian (4)	Christian—Catholic (3)	♥
Education	Some college	Some college (Associate's degree)	♥
Spending (1–4)	3	3	♥
Politics (1–4)	3	3	♥
Environment:			
▪ **Birth Order**	Lastborn of two (2 years younger than his older sibling)	Lastborn of five (8 years younger than her next-oldest sibling)	♥
▪ **Clean (1–4)**	2	2	♥
Chemistry	Type O	Type A	–
Togetherness	Kayaking, bowling, camping, watching movies, playing with our cats		♥
Matrix Score:			7

Both are Lastborns, somewhat liberal, fairly fastidious, aren't very religious or frugal, and have some college Education. They also list things they enjoy doing together that don't require too much planning ahead, including bowling, movies, and even kayaking. And whereas most couples in this study listed "travel" as a favorite Togetherness activity, Kathleen and Patrick specifically mention "camping," which makes for an easy weekend getaway whenever they need a couple of escape days.

And when it comes to Chemistry, hanging around together (indeed, Togetherness) is incredibly important in keeping the flame alive. After all, if you don't do anything together frequently, any Chemistry you felt at the beginning will fall flat.

Kathleen and Patrick are a great example of an A&O couple who have all of the other 7 factors in common—therefore, Perfect.

Profile C-8: Walt and Charlotte

I'd say 50 years of matrimony demonstrates a healthy marriage, wouldn't you? Even upon first glance at these two, the expression "two peas in a pod" comes to mind. Here is their Matrix:

	Walt	Charlotte	Matrix Points:
Religion (importance: 1–4)	Christian—Presbyterian (1)	Christian—Presbyterian (1)	♥
Education	Master's degree	Bachelor's degree	♥
Spending (1–4)	3	3	♥
Politics (1–4)	3	3	♥
Environment:			
▪ **Birth Order**	Firstborn of two	Firstborn of two	♥
▪ **Clean (1–4)**	2	2	♥
Chemistry	Type O	Type A	–
Togetherness	Playing bridge, playing games on the computer, being with friends		♥
Matrix Score:			7

Like Patrick and Kathleen, Charlotte and Walt earn a Perfect score of 7. They are a shining example of how a married couple needs those underlying commonalities of values and shared experiences. They are very active in their church, they both enjoy reading and intellectual interests, and they love telling about how they were almost crushed to death in a mob of people—and mouthed the words "I love you" to each other—while visiting Europe during their honeymoon!

Long story…but that's the point. In a good marriage, you'll get your own long stories and enjoy sharing them with others (as well as rehashing them with each other every so often) as you journey through life together.

Type B

General tendencies:
- Thinking-oriented, highly rational and logical
- Individualistic, nomadic, quietly gutsy, focused
- Easily make careless social errors
- Have minimal regard for time constraints
- Experts in their field, tend to have personal "trademarks"
- Well-rounded, extremely sober in personality behavior
- Hypercritical tendencies when out of balance
- Justice is extremely important
- Natural dairy eaters
- Superlative: Most Intellectual
- Beatitude: "Blessed are those who hunger and thirst for righteousness"

Author Peter Constantine calls Type Bs the "specialists"[4]; Dr. Peter D'Adamo calls them "sturdy and alert."[3] As a group, Type Bs are deliberate and well-rounded, and they especially shine in their field of expertise—and they tend to feel lost in areas that are new or uncomfortable. They exude intelligence because they naturally *specialize* in just a few things, so they do those things unusually well. And remember the Type A participant who told me he'd heard Type As described as "most popular"? Well, he'd also heard Type Bs are "least popular"! That makes sense, since Type Bs care the least about what others think of them—and they (we) shouldn't be too surprised that others have noticed that.

Type Bs can be rigid but make extremely devoted spouses, because they don't tend to be pulled in lots of different directions. Peter Constantine noted that they're "prone to blunders"[4] socially, but they usually develop strategies when they're young in order to compensate for this tendency—for example, they may learn that an open sense of humor can make up for their awkward moments. Type Bs set themselves apart naturally by having trademarks, whether it be their own fashion, phrases, interests, habits, or even foods.

As stated in the section about Type Os (with whom Type Bs tend to be very compatible), Type Bs are happiest with people with whom they can freely discuss a balance of the superficial (such as sports) and the thought-provoking (such as religion). Incidentally, Type Bs also tend to be winkers, but they wink to acknowledge someone in a "knowing" way rather than just being flirty.

111

The Goal

Type Bs tend to be most compatible with other Bs or with Type Os. (Not so much with Type As or ABs.) A typical Type B is on the introverted side but strives for balance, so a Type O who is independent and somewhat of a loner fills the bill wonderfully. Type Bs also tend to take themselves a little too seriously, but they demonstrate a casual flair that is unaffected by others' social status or economic position—and these traits naturally balance well with the Type O's openness, quick wit, and friendliness.

Similarly, a Type B who shares the same values and characteristics as another B will feel an amazing amount of Chemistry. The typical Type A or AB may feel uncomfortable with the B's tendency to react to situations without accounting for feelings, so Type B with either a Type A or AB is not usually a good combination—unless all seven of the other factors match. Type As and Bs usually have opposite inconsistencies: Type B being in thoughtful control but with a tendency to blurt out thoughts if it's seemingly justified and "the right thing to do," and Type A following what the others are doing and "not rocking the boat" while sometimes despising what they've agreed to do, and following rules stringently that they don't necessarily agree with.

Type Bs as a group are the least likely of the four types to be overweight, and they tend to have beautiful facial skin but not-so-good hair. (India has the highest per-capita percentage of Type Bs of all the countries—and picture them: They have beautiful skin, but the women pull their hair back.) Type Bs also easily get annoyed at people's quirks, but they are quick to overlook those quirks as long as the person is being kind. They aren't so quick to dismiss someone's bad personality as "just being how they are" like a Type O would, or to become good friends with them anyway, and give them private helpful feedback, like a Type A would.

The Type B's propensity toward "If…then" linear thinking is usually a good thing and is often interpreted as intelligence. However, it can get in the way of communicating with others—people aren't as predictable and logical as the Type B would like them to be!

The Type B's pragmatic nature makes them motivated to do well in the long term, planning future steps and moving (purposefully) one step at a time. The corresponding blind spot is that they don't always value the short term, so they're prone to take sudden missteps in social situations. But they get over it quickly, and they expect others to shrug it off with equal abandon. That's why they work so well with Type Os, who are the least likely to hold grudges.

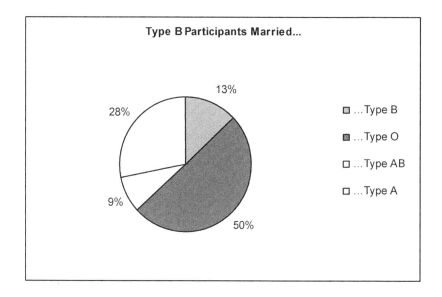

Figure C-3: Matrix Study Results of Type B Tendencies in Marriage

Looking even more deeply into the Type B statistics, the B&B marriages had the greatest *average* marriage endurance: 40 years (and all of them were still going at the time of this writing). Author Peter Constantine notes that Type Bs are probably too "individualistic" to find other Type Bs romantically on a frequent basis.[4] But I would add that when they do, the Chemistry is incredibly strong. This is also true of B&B friendships—when two Type Bs find each other as friends, they often feel like they're practically related. And their attraction to Type Os is unquestionable.

As explained later in this chapter under "Other Marriage Combinations," Type Bs were compatible with Type ABs as long as *both* were Firstborns or Only-Children—thus the relatively high 9% figure here with Type ABs.

Highly Compatible Marriage Combination: Type B and Type B

Profile C-9: Ray and Mary Lou

Although Type Bs don't find each other very often in marriage, we can cautiously deduce from the aforementioned 40-year average marriage that B&B couples, though rare, are highly successful. One such couple, Mary Lou and Ray, earn a Perfect score of 7 in their Matrix:

	Ray	Mary Lou	Matrix Points:
Religion (importance: 1–4)	Christian—Catholic (1)	Christian—Catholic (1)	♥
Education	Bachelor's degree	Bachelor's degree	♥
Spending (1–4)	1	4	–
Politics (1–4)	1	2	♥
Environment:			
▪ Birth Order	Firstborn of two	Firstborn of two	♥
▪ Clean (1–4)	2	1	♥
Chemistry	Type B	Type B	♥
Togetherness	Golf, travel, dinner, tennis, riding in the car		♥
Matrix Score:			7

Their only true point of contention is in financial matters, so they've developed techniques to avoid locking horns too much over money. Other than that, their Matrix corresponds beautifully across the board. After more than 38 years of marriage, their model has proven steadfast. (Insert lame joke here about Two B or not two B....)

Highly Compatible Marriage Combination: Type B and Type O

Profile C-10: Brian and Tracey

Both with their juris doctorates from law school, Tracey and Brian are a great example of a young couple who have similar backgrounds, perspectives, and values, as well as the highly compatible Chemistry combination of Type B and Type O.

They both describe themselves as devoted Christians, and they do go to church together; both are conservative; and both share many activities that they can enjoy every day. Her position as a Middle-Child makes her easily compatible with just about anyone (except an Only-Child or a Twin), but she is considerably more fastidious and more thrifty than he is. Still, they have plenty of similarities to keep things fun and interesting, plenty of ways to keep the marriage bond strong. Here is their Matrix:

	Brian	Tracey	Matrix Points:
Religion (importance: 1–4)	Christian— Methodist (1)	Christian— Catholic (1)	♥
Education	Juris doctorate (law school)	Juris doctorate (law school)	♥
Spending (1–4)	3	1	–
Politics (1–4)	2	1	♥
Environment:			
▪ **Birth Order**	Firstborn of two	Third of six (1 ½ years younger than her next-oldest sibling)	♥
▪ **Clean (1–4)**	3	1	–
Chemistry	Type O	Type B	♥
Togetherness	Golf, traveling, sports, watching movies and TV, playing cards, going out to dinner, talking, playing with our children		♥
Professional Extra Credit	Both are in the law profession		♥
Matrix Score:			7

Thanks to the Professional Extra Credit, these two lawyers earn a Perfect score of 7. We rest our case.

Type AB

General tendencies:
- A unique blend of A and B characteristics
- Extroverted when feeling confident
- Inconsistent
- Quietly disengage when sad or uncomfortable
- Make friends easily
- Like to build and create things wildly new
- Addictive tendencies when out of balance
- Enigmatic, photogenic, funny
- Natural herbivores and dairy eaters
- Superlative: Most Captivating
- Beatitude: "Blessed are the pure in heart"

115

Type AB, the rarest of the four types, has been described as the most "intriguing." Indeed, there's no such thing as an AB gene, as the only way for a person to be a Type AB is if they received a Type A gene from one parent and a Type B gene from the other. A person who's Type AB has some extreme gifts and extreme challenges that those of the other three blood groups don't generally have—at least, not all at once like ABs do. They have a purity of heart that isn't always understood or appreciated by others, so finding a good spouse is especially helpful toward the ultimate success of a Type AB.

ABs are outgoing like a Type O if they feel like they're in their element: They'll tell stories and jokes, and they'll be sensitive to the social dynamics around them. They're feelings-oriented like a Type A, but they also have a highly rational side and an often-impervious attitude toward others' opinions like a Type B. After all, Type AB was the last blood type to evolve, and it came into being when the Type A peoples and Type B peoples started to mix. So it makes sense that they're a little of everything.

One of the greatest challenges ABs have is to keep themselves in balance, and to steer themselves away from extremes—and this is probably why they do so well in marriage with Type As, given the A's gift for practicality and focus. Even the AB's health issues tend to more closely match that of Type As: For example, President John F. Kennedy was a Type AB, and it has been widely reported that he took medication for anxiety. Similarly, when Type As are out of balance, they can quickly become anxious.

Blood-type researchers tend to complain that there aren't enough Type ABs to study, so I aggressively recruited the Type ABs around me for this research. Incidentally, the Shroud of Turin has been tested to have the AB blood type. So if it really was Christ's burial cloth, every AB can feel duly honored.

The Goal

The naturally inherited Chemistry traits of Type AB include an obvious streak of independent-mindedness and a general (but guarded) zest for people. This combination makes them especially compatible with Type As as well as with fellow Type ABs. (Less so with Type Os or Bs.)

And as exemplified earlier in Profile C-3 (Michael and Susan), a **caveat** does exist in Type AB compatibility: They are indeed compatible with Type Os as long as one is a Firstborn and the other is a non-Firstborn. Every single AB&O couple in the Matrix survey had this combination of traits—and in most of them, the Type AB was the non-Firstborn and was the female, and the Type O was the Firstborn and was the male.

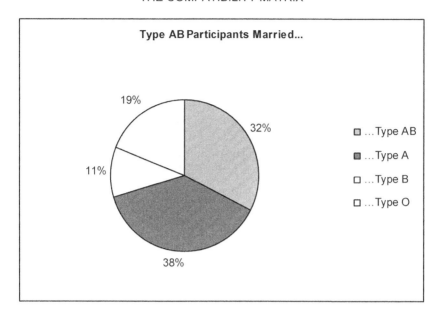

Figure C-4: Matrix Study Results of Type AB Marriages

Isn't the figure above fascinating, given that Type ABs represent only about 4% of the American population and Type Os represent about 48%? If blood type were a nonissue, this graph would show a much larger pie-piece of ABs matched up with Type O and a much, much smaller (if existent at all) pie-piece with other Type ABs.

As mentioned earlier, six couples in this survey who answered this question are both of the AB blood type. That's a binomial probability factor of .0016, or a chance of about 4 in 1,000,000. Having, say, one or two such couples in our sample size of 255 couples might have happened by coincidence, but not six. And the mutual attraction has been observed among friends as well: My friend Jon Gerler, a.k.a. DJ FM, remembers being in a college band where all four of them were Type ABs. Incredible.

Highly Compatible Marriage Combination: Type AB and Type AB

Profile C-11: Eric and Suzi

One of those six AB&AB couples, Suzi and Eric, have all the right commonalities for a lasting marriage. Looking at their Matrix, you can see their many similarities that give them a solid footing to begin with.

Even before they were married, Suzi and Eric endured the death of a family member together. Suzi explains: "My brother passed away when

[Eric and I] were both 20 years old—my brother committed suicide at the age of 25. This was an extremely traumatic event for both of us."

This sort of life-changing crisis tends to either bring two people closer together or push them apart. In their case, Suzi and Eric just grew closer and leaned on each other for comfort and support—after all, Eric had already started to get to know her family, so he felt the pain as well.

One thing to note is that they didn't get married *because* of their closeness that resulted from her brother's passing. Rather, they already had a strong bond based on basic similarities, and their relationship was "tested by fire." But just because someone is there for you during a life-altering circumstance doesn't mean that's the person you should marry; that's what friends are for. Here is their Matrix:

	Eric	Suzi	Matrix Points:
Religion (importance: 1–4)	Jewish/Christian— Baptist (3)	Christian— Lutheran (2)	♥
Education	Bachelor's degree	Bachelor's degree	♥
Spending (1–4)	1	2	♥
Politics (1–4)	3	3	♥
Environment:			
▪ Birth Order	Firstborn of two	Lastborn of four (5 years younger than her next-oldest sibling)	♥
▪ Clean (1–4)	3	2	♥
Chemistry	Type AB	Type AB	♥
Togetherness	Movies, games, long talks, long drives, traveling, going out for ice cream or out to eat		♥
Matrix Score:			8

She is Lutheran, and he was raised with one Jewish parent and one Baptist parent, so he is able to identify with her Protestant (Lutheran) upbringing. They both have their bachelor's degrees, both are frugal, and both are relatively liberal. He is a Firstborn, and she is a Virtual Firstborn; both are moderate in their Cleanliness expectations; and they were very effusive in listing their Togetherness activities.

If a trial like theirs happens to you while you're dating someone with whom you're becoming serious (or if it happens to the other person), allow some time to pass so you can mentally and emotionally step back and evaluate the big picture. And their big picture is an Ideal score of 8.

Highly Compatible Marriage Combination: Type AB and Type A

Profile C-12: James and Margaret

Speaking of the big picture, Margaret and James boast more than 50 years of marriage. (Fifty years!) Their union is yet another shining example of across-the-board compatibility.

Margaret and James have very strong Chemistry as an AB and A, respectively. ABs tend to favor their Type A side in sociability, generally preferring peacemaking (a Type A trait) above hard-nosed justice (a Type B trait), which is a huge reason why Type ABs tend to have a strong and lasting attraction with Type As. Here is their Matrix:

	James	Margaret	Matrix Points:
Religion (importance: 1–4)	Christian—Protestant (1)	Christian—Protestant (1)	♥
Education	Bachelor's degree	Bachelor's degree	♥
Spending (1–4)	4	3	♥
Politics (1–4)	2	3	♥
Environment:			
▪ **Birth Order**	Only-Child	Firstborn of four	♥
▪ **Clean (1–4)**	1	2	♥
Chemistry	Type A	Type AB	♥
Togetherness	Reading, traveling, volunteering, socializing with friends and family		♥
Matrix Score:			8

Margaret is the daughter of a Protestant minister, so it was important to her that she marry a Christian who shares her beliefs. They are both Firstborns, with James being a "super-Firstborn" as an Only-Child; they are also both politically moderate, educated with bachelor's degrees, relatively tidy, and not-so-frugal.

Incidentally, I have a particular vantage point of—and fondness for—the AB&A combination in marriage, because it also describes my own parents, my paternal grandparents, and several aunt-and-uncle sets. In my observation, this combination works very, very well.

Other Marriage Combinations: A&B, B&AB, and AB&O

The other three possible combinations can be fine in a marriage as long as the couple has all of the other seven factors in the Matrix scale well aligned—and the following quirks were noted during the Matrix study:

Type A and Type B

The quirk that can make this work: All of the A&B married couples in the Matrix survey ranked Religion for themselves as a 1 or 2. (None of these individuals ranked themselves as a 3 or 4—absolutely none of them.) Therefore, if Religion is ranked as a 1 or 2 by both persons in an A&B couple, then they can give themselves a point for Chemistry on the Matrix scale. (Note that this wasn't a trend with other combinations.)

In fact, this group included the only Jewish participant in this study to rank Religion as a 1 in importance (Brian in Profile R-5, who is Type B), and this group also included a Hindu adherent (another Type B man). A person's Religion tends to value the individual's beliefs and, which usually follows, one-on-one relationships (between you and God). So this trend makes sense in light of both Type A's and Type B's tendency toward being attracted to introspection and intellectual pursuits, rather than frequent get-togethers with groups for purely social purposes: If they're going to be with a group, in their minds, it's better to be doing something that's purposeful and meaningful—such as a worship service or charity work.

The A&B couples in the survey displayed a tendency to emphasize their shared similarities, which seems to indicate that these couples don't include extremes of either side: The Type B in this type of marriage tended to be more of a people-pleaser than your typical B, and/or the Type A tended to be more individualistic than a typical Type A.

While Types A and B are both on the introverted side of the scale and both enjoy pursuits whereby you *evaluate* things, the Type A will be more of a people-pleaser and will say things just to keep the peace—which can be frustrating to the Type B, who will expect independent-mindedness and straightforward truth. Peacemaking and justice are sometimes at odds with each other in this world, after all.

So Religion is the factor that can create evenness between the two; be careful if that's not the case. (Again, this is the case with the A&B combination only.)

Type B and Type AB

The quirk that can make this work: All of the B&AB couples in the Matrix survey comprised Firstborns or Only-Children married to other

Firstborns or Only-Children. Therefore, it appears that the B&AB combination works together just fine as long as *both* partners are Firstborns or Only-Children; if this is the case, they can give themselves a point for Chemistry on the Matrix scale. (Remember that the firstborn male in a family *can* render the man to have Firstborn characteristics.)

Type Bs like predictability and balance, whereas ABs can sometimes be unpredictable and get off-balance easily. That said, these types are both moderate when it comes to introversion/extroversion: Type B being mildly introverted, Type AB mildly extroverted. (Type ABs will probably bristle at the thought that they might be pinned as "mildly extroverted," as they don't really like to be pegged in any which way!)

Interestingly, none of the participants who are in B&AB marriages rated themselves as a 1 in Religious importance (the opposite of the A&B couples mentioned above!), which might have to do with both types' general bent toward doing their own thing and being extremely independent.

So being the Firstborn child in a family is the factor that can create evenness between a Type B and a Type AB; be careful if that's not the case. (Again, this is the case with the B&AB combination only.)

Type AB and Type O

The quirk that can make this work: The AB&O couples in the Matrix study demonstrated three odd consistencies with Birth Order trends:
- *First* (and most importantly), every single one of these couples comprised a **Firstborn** (or an Only-Child) who married **anything but another Firstborn** (or Only-Child).
- *Second*, all but one of these **Firstborns were the Type Os** in their marriages. In other words, among the AB&O couples in the Matrix study, the Type O was the Firstborn—and therefore the AB was the non-Firstborn—in almost all of these marriages.
- *Third*, all but one of the **Firstborns in this group were the males**. In other words, among our AB&O couples, the Type O was the male—and therefore the AB was the female—in almost all of these marriages.

Therefore, we can safely conclude that the AB&O combination can work very well as long as one partner is a Firstborn and the other isn't. And ideally, though not as necessary, the Type O is the Firstborn and is also the male. The gender factor seems to be the least important of the three. Again, this is the *opposite* of what we noted in the B&AB couples mentioned above! Read about an O&AB couple in Profile C-3 (Michael and Susan) earlier in this chapter.

So this special condition of Birth Order is the factor that can create evenness between a Type AB and a Type O. (Again, this is the case with the AB&O combination only.)

The Bottom Line on A&B, B&AB, and AB&O Couples

These statistics seem to show an interesting combination of traits that blend well together or not. AB does well with B if both are independent Firstborns; AB does well with O if one spouse is a Firstborn and the other is a non-Firstborn; and A does well with B if they share intensely similar perspectives on Religion and spirituality. If so, they can give themselves a point for Chemistry on the Matrix scale.

Final Thoughts on Chemistry...

I always wince when I tell someone about the blood type connection to personality and they say, "Oh! Just like astrology!" On the contrary: The patterns of blood type begin to prove out the Creator's purposeful manipulation of human chemistry as people moved to different climates and ate new foods—lest they all die out. Those same patterns haven't changed at the cellular level, and they've been passed on for generations with the revised programming intact, which are accompanied by behavioral/attitudinal tendencies that survived along with them.

That's why the blood type connection with personality doesn't offend me as a religious person, because it has nothing to do with chance and everything to do with purposeful, thoughtful, loving creation of an individual. You.

It's not too hard to envision that the hunter-gatherer Type Os had to be loud and aggressive in a successful hunt, the agrarian-society Type As had to get along with neighbors and be okay with working quietly and diligently at the task of farming, and the animal-domestication and cold-climate Type Bs had to be able to persevere amid adverse physical conditions and, likely, therefore not get too personal about things (it's hard to be warm when you're cold!). Type AB is a combination of A and B traits.

So we each tend to be compatible with certain people biochemically, and these are the Chemistry trends observed in this survey. It has nothing to do with when you were born on the yearly calendar—as First Baptist Church of Atlanta pastor Charles Stanley once said in a sermon, "Horoscope should be spelled horror-scope!" I like that. Blood type has purpose, it's a special part of your individual design; birthday is just an indicator of where the Earth was positioned relative to the sun when you were born. It's fun, but it doesn't deserve any deeper consideration.

And blood type is only the tip of the iceberg. As the human genome is mapped and analyzed, intellectually open-minded scientists are writing that living beings are too purposefully designed to have been a happenstance of the cosmos—of atoms crashing against one another and somehow organizing. Indeed, Francis S. Collins, former head of the Human Genome Project, has written "The Language of God: A Scientist Presents Evidence for Belief" (Simon & Schuster, 2006), delineating his own path from atheism to Christianity through his scientific observations. Even outside the realm of science, anyone who has ever worked on a project (of any kind) knows that the project wouldn't get done if all the tools just sat on the table or blew around in a vacuum. There has to be effort and thought behind the completion of anything, otherwise it remains a mess and is certainly not organized. So the thought that a Creator created you on purpose, with all of your idiosyncrasies and gifts, isn't so far-fetched.

If you're an intelligent person but you think the Chemistry theory is bogus, I invite you to observe the happy couples around you who you know personally: Do they score a 7 or 8 on the Matrix scale? Chances are they do. And even if the Chemistry factor is off for one of these happy couples in your midst, they do indeed have enough in common to score a 7 on the Matrix scale. Otherwise, their level of **happiness** wouldn't be as high as it should be. And after all, isn't happiness the point of finding the right person? If not—if marriage is only a means toward having children or scoring points of propriety—forget it.

People who are best friends with someone of the opposite sex sometimes rationalize that they should just go ahead and marry each other, even if there's no true (mutual) physical attraction between them. But this usually results in divorce, so let's avoid that—make sure you're both physically attracted to each other, and that there's no feeling of compulsion. (If you have to really think about this, the answer is probably no.)

We can learn from everyone, but we can't live with everyone. You're looking for someone with whom you'll ideally live for the rest of your life, and so it's incredibly important to feel attracted to each other. And blood type is one way of measuring and analyzing this attraction.

If you'd like to learn a little more about the biology behind blood types, see the summary in Chapter 8 Appendix: Blood Type Biology toward the end of this book.

~ Cheat Sheet ~	
RESPE**C**T	**Answer: People who are… Should look for…**
Chemistry: Blood type	**Type Os…** other Type Os or Type Bs **Type As…** other Type As or Type ABs **Type Bs…** other Type Bs or Type Os **Type ABs…** other Type ABs or Type As

RESPEC̲T:

Chapter 9: T̲ogetherness

What are your favorite activities to do?	(List the things you enjoy doing regularly:)

"Constant togetherness is fine—but only for Siamese twins."
— Victoria Billings

Why This Is Important

If you and the person you're dating have compatible RESPEC_ qualities but don't enjoy some of the same daily or weekly activities, the relationship will fall apart. After all, why would you want to spend the rest of your life with (and have children with) someone you don't even like to hang out with?

The survey's divorced participants didn't have much to say regarding things they enjoyed doing together—the Togetherness question was usually left blank altogether. This is incredibly significant.

The Goal

Who you're most compatible with: In Togetherness, you're looking for someone who enjoys the same sorts of activities as you do. Not all day every day, but there should be plenty of things you both enjoy doing together and activities you enjoy talking about.

The Togetherness factor includes enjoying meals the same way, enjoying some (but not necessarily all) of the same sorts of activities together on weekends, and having similar patterns.

One divorcée told me about how much she loves going to plays—so much so that she'll go by herself. After she got married, she realized that her new husband hated plays, so she continued to go alone. In fact, they had a hard time finding *anything* they enjoyed doing together. So the marriage fizzled out within 2 years.

As a marriage grows stronger, you enjoy each other's company and the "routine" even more—even if the routine is to grab the boat or kayak out of storage at whim and go tooling around the lake on a Saturday. If this sort of spontaneity is your cup of tea, you would be best suited with someone who likes this sort of thing as well. If, however, an ideal Saturday would include breakfast or lunch together, a walk somewhere, and maybe a nap in the sunshine or even a matinee, then you should look for someone who enjoys those things.

This isn't to say you have to do everything together, but you should easily be able to spend quality time with each other on a regular basis, doing things you both enjoy—regardless of the activity. It can be active or passive, social or not social. If you enjoy reading books and magazines and newspapers on the weekends, you two can probably both enjoy reading in the same room. It's important to be with each other, and have access to each other, on a daily basis, and for your activities to be natural and not forced.

There's no pie chart for this one, because only a handful of couples didn't answer this question; the ones who said they don't do anything together are indeed not very happy together, so they're probably just trudging along in marriage because it's easier and cheaper to stay married than to get divorced. Ugh! Let's try to avoid that, shall we?

Togetherness must be a "given" if you're going to marry someone. You need to have things you enjoy doing together to help maintain a happy relationship. And just sleeping together doesn't count—you should enjoy some (but not all) of the same "free-time" activities when you're first together, because those activities will increase and evolve over time as you're together longer.

Profile T-1: Ted and Diane

For the Togetherness question, both Diane and Ted wrote "sports" and "movies," then Ted added "TV" and Diane put "vegging"—which probably mean the same thing: vegging in front of the TV together! All four of these activities are easy, low-maintenance pastimes that can be enjoyed daily or weekly, so theirs is a wonderful answer.

	Ted	Diane	Matrix Points:
Religion (importance: 1–4)	Christian— Protestant (3)	Christian— Methodist (2)	♥
Education	High school diploma	Some college	♥
Spending (1–4)	3	1	–
Politics (1–4)	3	4	♥
Environment:			
▪ Birth Order	Lastborn of three (5 years younger than his next-oldest sibling)	Third of five (2 years younger than her next-oldest sibling)	♥
▪ Clean (1–4)	2	2	♥
Chemistry	Type O	Type B	♥
Togetherness	Sports, movies, watching TV, vegging		♥
Matrix Score:			7

Diane and Ted score a Perfect 7, with their only disparate factor being in the Spending arena. But after more than 16 years of marriage, they've figured out how to deal with that issue. These two Thirdborns earn first prize in compatibility.

Profile T-2: David and Trudy

One of my favorite instructors at the University of Florida's College of Journalism, David taught us practical lessons he learned as founder of "Wichita City Life" magazine. He was also a Methodist minister, plus he and his wife actually ran a circus every summer!

David passed away due to an extended illness just a few months after I graduated, but his wife has kept me posted about all the fun times she continues to have with her friends through their churches and the circus. They were married for 27 years.

Trudy and David certainly had myriad projects and various initiatives constantly on their plate! They loved doing these projects together, and Trudy is the consummate glowing pastor's wife with a fresh smile for everyone.

Even though we don't know what David's blood type was, they have a Perfect score of 7 anyway, and we could almost even give them Professional Extra Credit for running that circus together. They're aligned in Religion, Education, Spending, Politics, Environment (both Birth Order and Cleanliness), and Togetherness. Here is their Matrix:

	David	Trudy	Matrix Points:
Religion (importance: 1–4)	Christian—Methodist (1)	Christian—Methodist (1)	♥
Education	Doctorate	Bachelor's degree	♥
Spending (1–4)	3	2	♥
Politics (1–4)	3	3	♥
Environment:			
▪ Birth Order	Only-Child	Firstborn of three	♥
▪ Clean (1–4)	2	2	♥
Chemistry	(not available)	Type O	–
Togetherness	Running the circus, being in the car traveling together		
Matrix Score:			7

Their enjoyment of lots of Togetherness activities together, and shared perspectives and values, made for a shining example of marriage that works "'til death do us part." And they lived happily ever after.

Profile T-3: Bert and Katia

She lived in Colombia; he was in The Netherlands. "This was back when the first chat rooms appeared, and the Internet really was something very new to a lot of people," said Katia. "So it was pretty innocent back then. There were only about 30 people chatting [in English], and we all knew each other—very different from the stuff you see nowadays!"

I was struck by how they answered the Togetherness question: "Everything!!! (Even nothing)" speaks volumes about how they keep their relationship strong, and in a very natural way: Even if they're just hanging out together and doing "nothing," they're enjoying each other's company. They're best friends.

Katia and Bert's transcontinental online relationship lasted for about a year before Bert took a trip around the world with a buddy, ending the journey in Colombia to finally meet Katia. She says that they immediately knew they were soul mates.

Here is their Matrix:

	Bert	Katia	Matrix Points:
Religion (importance: 1–4)	Christian— Protestant (4)	Christian— Catholic (4)	♥
Education	Master's degree	Bachelor's degree	♥
Spending (1–4)	2	2	♥
Politics (1–4)	3	3	♥
Environment:			
▪ Birth Order	Lastborn of three (4 years younger than his next-oldest sibling)	Lastborn of two (5 years younger than her older sibling)	♥
▪ Clean (1–4)	2	1	♥
Chemistry	Type O	Type O	♥
Togetherness	"Everything!!! (Even nothing)"		♥
Matrix Score:			8

Note that Bert and Katia's relationship evolved *naturally*. Their mutual attraction wasn't forced, and it didn't happen amid peer pressure. On your own personal quest, really think and be aware of relationships with other people that make you feel comfortable—the people who make you feel like you don't have to put on airs, or to schedule unnatural events in order to enjoy each other's company. You should feel comfortable and happy while eating a meal together or talking on the phone. But if you're dating someone with whom your phone calls and meals together just cause awkward silence (silence is fine, awkwardness is not), it's time to move on.

The Environment, Chemistry, and Togetherness factors are where your *comfort* with others really comes out. When developing deep relationships, you'll find yourself drawn to people who understand your general modus operandi and whose m.o. you'll understand as well.

Profile T-4: Robbie and Kay

Living close to the Atlantic Ocean, these two cited that they enjoy diving, fishing, and watching sports. Far from the image of a woman thumbing her nose at sports, Kay reflects a definite trend among survey participants: Men who enjoy watching sports tend to marry women who enjoy watching sports! (Pay attention, guys!)

Not every man enjoys watching sports, so a woman who really doesn't like sports at all should marry a man who either feels the same way or watches infrequently. Most women who are happily married to frequent sports-watchers learn to (or already do) enjoy watching her husband's favorite sport, at least to a small degree (i.e., not with nagging criticism about his watching). Here is their Matrix:

	Robbie	Kay	Matrix Points:
Religion (importance: 1–4)	Christian— Presbyterian (2)	Christian— Presbyterian (2)	♥
Education	Bachelor's degree	Bachelor's degree	♥
Spending (1–4)	3	3	♥
Politics (1–4)	2	3	♥
Environment:			
▪ Birth Order	Third of five (2 years younger than his next-oldest sibling)	Firstborn of two	♥
▪ Clean (1–4)	3	1	–
Chemistry	Type A	Type A	♥
Togetherness	Watching sports, scuba diving, "Fishing for big fish" (him), "Fishing for little fish" (her)		♥
Matrix Score:			7

Rolling Stone magazine contributing editor Touré mused on CNN about why Academy Award–winning actress Halle Berry ever married professional baseball player David Justice in the first place. (The couple were divorced at the time of the broadcast.) "She doesn't even *like* baseball!" he said incredulously. "If you don't like baseball, you shouldn't marry a baseball player."

It seems so obvious, doesn't it? But when the sparks of attraction are flying, it's *not* obvious. And that's why marriage needs to be about more than physical attraction (more than just Chemistry), more than superficial commonalities like race and popularity. You need to be able to enjoy several different bonding activities together on a regular basis (weekly and daily)— like watching sports, eating dinner, or simply reading in the same room.

Profile T-5: Charles and Bea

As we grow older (better!) and less active (less stressed!), our Togetherness activities naturally change. Bea and Charles have fun golfing, playing bingo, and reading together. Here is their Matrix:

	Charles	Bea	Matrix Points:
Religion (importance: 1–4)	Christian—Presbyterian (1)	Christian—Presbyterian (1)	♥
Education	Bachelor's degree	Some college	♥
Spending (1–4)	2	1	♥
Politics (1–4)	1	1	♥
Environment:			
▪ Birth Order	Only-Child	Second of two (1 year younger than her next-oldest sibling)	–
▪ Clean (1–4)	1	1	♥
Chemistry	Type O	Type O	♥
Togetherness	Golf, reading, church, bingo, watching TV		♥
Matrix Score:			7

If two people enjoy similar activities when they're young, they'll enjoy corresponding hobbies and entertainment pastimes when they're older, too. But even mature marriages require shared basic values and commonalities, and Bea and Charles earn a Perfect score of 7. Bingo!

Spouses in the Spotlight Due to Fame or High-Profile Jobs

People who have high-visibility jobs, such as politicians, pastors, executives, actors, and athletes, are scrutinized *socially* on a somewhat regular basis. At the end of a hard day in such a profession, this extends beyond the need to simply unwind and maybe complain about a slacking coworker. They must unload emotionally as well, and the spouse must be willing and able to commiserate and to really listen.

If you're developing a serious relationship with someone who is or will be in the spotlight, consider whether your daily conversations (which are integral to Togetherness) will be what you're comfortable with, and whether you can tolerate listening to all the crazy conflicts your spouse has to deal with…and whether you, yourself, have the tolerance to endure scrutiny you don't deserve, or if you think it would make you too paranoid.

A quintessential example is the First Lady of the United States, who receives collateral scrutiny and intrusive questioning simply because of the high-profile nature of her spouse's job. If the spouse's fame is more local than national, the circumstances are nevertheless a microcosm of the

First Lady's situation. So while it may seem glamorous at first to marry a high-profile person, consider whether or not you have the wherewithal to enjoy that scrutinized lifestyle.

Final Thoughts on Togetherness…

"Doesn't everybody do that?" asked Mary Lou, when I asked her (for clarification) which soap opera it was that she and her husband always watch together. They watch "The Young and the Restless" every afternoon.

No, not everybody does that, but we all have our own "Doesn't everybody do that" expectations/assumptions. So whatever your own version of "Doesn't everybody do that" is, whether it be getting take-out every night for dinner, living on a large farm, going to church every Sunday and Wednesday…you do have your own "Doesn't everybody do that." Make sure you marry someone who does do that, whatever "that" is for you.

Whereas you can discuss Religion, Education, Spending, Politics, Environment (both Birth Order and Cleanliness), and even Chemistry over e-mail or the phone, you need to actually experience how it **feels** to hang around together when it comes to Togetherness. Togetherness is why the dating process itself is so important—because general habits and expectations will come out.

Be aware of awkward scenarios that play out, especially as the two of you decide what to do together the next time you go out. And don't downplay your own expectations and habits: If your ideal Saturday is to sleep in late and have a leisurely lunch, don't marry someone who would rather have a big breakfast early in the morning, skip lunch, and take Rover to the dog park all afternoon. Such oppositeness becomes glaringly clear the longer you date someone who is too different from you. But if you do like Rover, go ahead and give it a chance at the park—and if it turns out that you hate this habit, it's better to let that dating relationship end. And don't fake it. Faking it will only result in a failed or unhappy marriage.

Remember Ken and Sheryle, from Profile R-2 in the Religion chapter? They have their Saturdays mapped out in a way that they both enjoy, and they never get tired of the routine—it's always fun and rewarding in a new way, every week. Likewise, consider your own habits, activities, and things you like to do, and find someone who enjoys those things, too.

~ Cheat Sheet ~	
RESPEC_T_	**Answer:**
Togetherness: Activities	…Look for someone who enjoys some of the same activities as you do, during the week and on weekends

Chapter 10: Cheat Sheet & Romance Tracker

Hint: Refer to the end of each RESPECT chapter for your answers!

Cheat Sheet	Myself	All Possible Traits of MY Ideal Mate (for reference):
Religion or affiliation? 1–4?	Importance: 1= Very; 4=Not very: 1 2 3 4	Importance: 1= Very; 4=Not very: 1 2 3 4
Highest **education** level/degree completed?	☐ Jr. High School ☐ High School ☐ Some College/ Associate's ☐ Bachelor's ☐ Master's ☐ Doctorate	☐ Jr. High School ☐ High School ☐ Some College/ Associate's ☐ Bachelor's ☐ Master's ☐ Doctorate
Spending (frugalness)?	1=Very; 4=Not very: 1 2 3 4	1=Very; 4=Not very: 1 2 3 4
Political bent?	1=Conservative; 4=Liberal: 1 2 3 4	1=Conservative; 4=Liberal: 1 2 3 4
Environment (1): Birth order/role in the family?	☐ Only-Child ☐ Firstborn of ___ ☐ Middle child, number ___ of ___; my next-oldest sibling was ___ years older than I, and my next-youngest sibling was ___ years younger than I ☐ Lastborn of ___; my next-oldest sibling was ___ years older than I	☐ Only-Child ☐ Firstborn of ___ ☐ Middle child, number ___ of ___; their next oldest sibling was ___ years older, and their next-youngest sibling was ___ years younger ☐ Lastborn of ___; their next-oldest sibling was ___ years older
Environment (2): Neat/clean?	1=Very; 4=Not very: 1 2 3 4	1=Very; 4=Not very: 1 2 3 4
Chemistry: Blood type?	O A B AB	O A B AB
Togetherness activities?		

Romance Tracker© …"Their" side of the Matrix as you date... (Make a few copies of this page for yourself only)	Name: On: ___ / ___ / ___ Where we went: Thoughts: Contact info:	Name: On: ___ / ___ / ___ Where we went: Thoughts: Contact info:
Religion or affiliation? 1–4?	Importance: 1= Very; 4=Not very: 1 2 3 4	Importance: 1= Very; 4=Not very: 1 2 3 4
Highest **education** level/degree completed?	☐ Jr. High School ☐ High School ☐ Some College/ 　　Associate's ☐ Bachelor's ☐ Master's ☐ Doctorate	☐ Jr. High School ☐ High School ☐ Some College/ 　　Associate's ☐ Bachelor's ☐ Master's ☐ Doctorate
Spending (frugalness)?	1=Very; 4=Not very: 1 2 3 4	1=Very; 4=Not very: 1 2 3 4
Political bent?	1=Conservative; 4=Liberal: 1 2 3 4	1=Conservative; 4=Liberal: 1 2 3 4
Environment: Birth order/role in the family?	☐ Only-Child ☐ Firstborn of ___ ☐ Middle child, 　　number ___ of ___; 　　their next-oldest 　　sibling was ___ years 　　older, and their next- 　　youngest sibling was 　　___ years younger ☐ Lastborn of ___; the 　　next-oldest sibling 　　was ___ years older	☐ Only-Child ☐ Firstborn of ___ ☐ Middle child, 　　number ___ of ___; 　　their next-oldest 　　sibling was ___ years 　　older, and their next- 　　youngest sibling was 　　___ years younger ☐ Lastborn of ___; the 　　next-oldest sibling 　　was ___ years older
Environment: Neat/clean?	1=Very; 4=Not very: 1 2 3 4	1=Very; 4=Not very: 1 2 3 4
Chemistry: Blood type?	O A B AB	O A B AB
Togetherness activities?		

Chapter 11: Lesser Issues in Compatibility

There are several areas in which people tend to make general opinions about others without considering the individual. Don't listen to the naysayers, because the fact is that if you approach the Mr/s. Right–finding mission with the RESPECT list rather than society's list (racial lines, age lines, etc.), you will be on your individualized track—as opposed to fulfilling others' expectations and guidelines. Marriage is an individualized institution, not a group institution. We don't marry a group of people.

Race

Several couples in the survey were of different races, and they get along just as well as do the other happy marriages in the study. No surprise there.

Profile L-1: Kehinde and Kathryn

Kathryn and Kehinde have been happily married for more than 6 years. They have the cutest return-address labels that feature cartoon-style faces of themselves, as well as of their daughter, and their cat and fish...adorable! This cartoon shows a swarthy-complexioned man and a white woman.

Look at how low-maintenance their Togetherness activities are—things they can enjoy every day, not just on the weekends or on vacation. And Kehinde is a Twin, which meshes well with Kathryn's upbringing as a Lastborn. Their only area of tension might be the Cleanliness factor, so they must have figured out how to work past that—but they're an optimum fit in everything else. Here is their Matrix:

	Kehinde	Kathryn	Matrix Points:
Religion (importance: 1–4)	Christian—Catholic (2)	Christian—Catholic (2)	♥
Education	Master's degree	Bachelor's degree	♥
Spending (1–4)	3	2	♥
Politics (1–4)	2	3	♥
Environment:			
▪ Birth Order	Twin—sixth of eight (3 years younger than his non-twin older sibling)	Lastborn of two (2 years younger than her older sibling)	♥
▪ Clean (1–4)	4	1	–
Chemistry	Type O	Type B	♥
Togetherness	Walking, singing, dancing, watching TV, movies, sports events, going to the gym		♥
Matrix Score:			7

Their score of 7 showcases their harmonized life together. Perfect!

Age

Several couples in the study have large age gaps (10 years or more), and these marriages showed the same patterns of shared characteristics as everyone else.

In a successful age-gap marriage, the younger of the two is usually very mature in character, as Joe Christiano said in the Foreword about his own wife. As long as the age difference doesn't create unattraction from the perspective of the younger one or a feeling of superiority by the older one, and they have at least 7 of the possible 8 Matrix factors in line with each other, there shouldn't be a problem.

Profile L-2: James and Nadine

James was a 20-year-old entrepreneur when he bought a comic-book store, and there he met 30-year-old Nadine—one of the store's regular customers. They've now been married more than 20 years, and here is their Matrix:

135

	James	Nadine	Matrix Points:
Religion (importance: 1–4)	None given (4)	None given (3)	♥
Education	Some college	Bachelor's degree	♥
Spending (1–4)	2	2	♥
Politics (1–4)	3	3	♥
Environment:			
▪ Birth Order	Only-Child	Firstborn of three	♥
▪ Clean (1–4)	2	2	♥
Chemistry	Type O	Type A	–
Togetherness	Movies, reading, walking, vacations, TV, music		♥
Matrix Score:			7

As evidenced by the way they met, Nadine and James truly enjoy the same types of entertainment, including movies and comic books, and this is especially important to both of them. Both are generally nonreligious and are self-described liberal Democrats, and both are Firstborns—James being a "super-Firstborn" as an Only-Child. The only factor that isn't a match is their Chemistry, but interestingly, Nadine's father was a Type O like James; her mother is a Type A, so Nadine's marriage reflects her parents' marriage. And all their other 7 factors are indeed very well aligned with each other. Applause to Nadine and James!

Profile L-3: Boaz and Ruth

The book of Ruth in the Bible tells the story of King David's great-grandmother, and how this Moabite woman (that's right, she wasn't Jewish) became a revered ancestor to David and thereby Jesus as well. Being the marvelously über-suprahuman poet that God is, He had her marry into a Jewish family—but she didn't marry Boaz.

Ruth married a Jewish man whose family had moved to Moab from Bethlehem. But after they were married for 10 years, tragedy struck—her husband died, and so did his brother. Ruth's mother-in-law, Naomi, who had been widowed for a while, decided to go back to Bethlehem to try to find distant relatives she could live with, because now the family had no male anchors to keep them stable and secure. She told her daughters-in-law to go back to their own parents' homes; Naomi was able to convince her daughter-in-law Orpah (yes, Oprah Winfrey is named after her!), but Ruth refused to leave Naomi—and in one of the most frequently quoted passages of love and loyalty in the Old Testament, Ruth tells Naomi, "For wherever you go, I will go, and wherever you live, I will live; your people will be my people, and your God will be my God."

So Naomi and Ruth went to Bethlehem, and Naomi told Ruth to go glean from the fields to get some food. The field Ruth happened to glean from was owned by Boaz, one of the members of Naomi's husband's family! I'll let you read the whole juicy story yourself (the whole book is barely four pages long), but suffice it to say that Boaz was attracted to Ruth when he saw her, and he asked his servants who she was. Boaz had already heard through the grapevine about Ruth's loyalty to her mother-in-law, so he already held a deep respect for her even before he met her in his fields.

And they indeed had a considerable age difference: He said to her, "You have shown [even] more kindness than before, because you have not pursued younger men."

So Boaz married Ruth, and they had a son named Obed—father of Jesse, the father of King David. Naomi was thrilled to become a grandmother after all, which she thought was impossible after losing both of her sons. And they lived happily ever after.

Such is how it's supposed to be with marriage. It's magical! I love how this story is completely devoid of modern cynicism. It's a beautiful display of absolute purity and kindness and love.

The saying is true: "Age is important only when one is choosing wine or cheese." Still, as we'll learn from Charles and Susan (Profile D-4 in Chapter 13: Why Some Marriages Don't Work Out), sometimes there can be an intrigue or infatuation that proves out to be quite shallow over time. Again, that's why taking time to go through the dating process with each other helps flesh out the initial shock of romantic attraction you both felt at the beginning. If it's real, it'll last.

Morning Doves and Night Owls

One of the questions in the survey asked people to identify themselves as a morning person or a night owl. Some people truly identify themselves as naturally "waking up at the crack of dawn" or "staying up past midnight," so this question was aimed to find out whether this was a shared trait among couples.

But there wasn't much of a trend. Morning people were almost as likely to marry night owls as they were to marry other morning doves, and vice versa—53% of couples were the same as each other in this area, but 47% were opposites. So unless you'd be almost *offended* if the other person didn't tiptoe around your sleep schedule, this is probably a nonissue.

"Personality Type"

The introversion/extroversion factor isn't quite aligned with compatibility. In the Matrix survey, I asked people to define themselves as the "A" personality type (high-energy/intense) or "B" personality type (relaxed/calm), or somewhere in the middle. One problem with this turned out to be that people don't always characterize themselves in the same way that others might—perhaps they're not very intuitive, or perhaps they are prejudicial in that they value one personality type over the other—so they **identify** with that type regardless of whether it actually reflects their own personality. So this turned out to be too sticky to really quantify, and thus it's a nonissue.

However, it was consistently observed that "talkers" tended to marry "listeners." In other words, people who love to talk and entertain others tend to marry people who like to listen and be entertained. But there isn't a good way to quantify and measure this, especially when people are young. The best way to judge is through experience, and that's why it's so important to date each other and see how you two jibe.

If you're on a date and you're annoyed by how "quiet" the other person is, you need to look for a talker, because you're not naturally filling the void; alternatively, if you feel that the other person is a chatterbox and never lets you get a word in edgewise, you need to look for more of a listener. In fact, men who think of all women as chatterboxes need to date listener-type women, and women who think that men always dominate the conversation need to find listener-type men. Sometimes people don't date the right types of people! It's pretty simple, but it does require dating various types of people to see what your preference is.

Pay attention to the people who make you smile a lot and feel good about yourself. That's the type you're looking for.

Personal Family History/Trauma

In the survey, I asked participants whether they'd experienced a traumatic family event before the age of 22, whether it be the death of someone close to them, the divorce of their own parents, or other. Most people who cited that they did indeed have such an experience were not married to someone who shared this background—i.e., people who had experienced the divorce of their parents were equally as likely to marry someone whose parents also divorced as they were to marry someone whose parents had stayed together, and those who had experienced the death of a close friend or relative were rarely married to someone who had gone through the same thing.

A notable exception is the marriage of Kevin and Kara in Profile Env-Birth-7 (in the Environment chapter under "Birth Order"), who each experienced the death of their father at a young age. So, it is certainly a good thing to tie the knot with someone who can empathize with you, but complete experience-based empathy in this area isn't imperative.

Children and Pets

It may be hard to believe that two people who are madly in love and have all the right things in common could possibly have heated arguments over kids or pets. But such is life, and it's a good idea to discuss these issues beforehand, to get them out of the way. Just like with issues such as Religion, you shouldn't enter the covenant of marriage with the thought that you'll "talk them into" having children, or that you'll definitely have dogs or cats regardless of what your spouse says. Marriage isn't a dictatorship, it's the most advanced form of friendship.

Discuss it first, and come up with a compromise that you both can live with. After all, one great character-builder in marriage is that you learn (out of sheer motivation) how to compromise, so the one who's getting their own way in one area is probably naturally giving into or giving up something else—in another issue—for the other.

Plus, in a strong marriage, the couple becomes more like-minded as the relationship grows deeper, and minds can change. And it may be your own!

Miscellaneous Lesser Issues

One woman, Melissa, used to tell me about how she tends to like left-handed men, because she herself is left-handed. But it's a good thing that she wasn't too strict with her theory, because she ended up falling in love with and marrying a right-handed man.

It's fun to think about certain quirks we have and to imagine that maybe our match will have the same quirk. But fun is all that is, so don't get stuck on whimsical theories—they're usually fun but not very deep. The RESPECT Principle is about matching up in mind, body, and spirit—not in superficial ways that don't really matter in the long run.

Chapter 12: Second Marriages

Even if you've already been married before, don't lower your standards if you're looking to possibly tie the knot again. Some people have had such a horrible first marriage that they're eager just to find a nice, level-headed person who treats them well—so they lower their standards. But it's important to have the same basic values, perspectives, and expectations.

Remember Kenneth and Dorothy (Profile Edu-2) in the Education chapter? They were each widowed and then "found each other," and they have an Ideal score of 8. They were fussy! It's a great lesson in how rewarding it is to find the right match, even the second time around.

Marriage After Divorce

Profile SM-1: George and Rose

Rose and George were both in their late 40s, recently divorced and each with two grown children, when they met. Rose was new in town, hired for a high position on the local school board; a reporter came to interview her for an article about her for the newspaper. The next day, the reporter came back to tell her that the house she bought happened to be right next-door to George, the publisher of the paper.

When they met each other for the first time, Rose and George were standing in front of their homes, and they shook hands—and didn't let go for about 5 minutes. Within the week, they went on a date, and they talked about everything from Religion to Politics to art and music during the 40-minute drive to the restaurant. "By the end of that 40 minutes, we knew we'd be married," says Rose.

They were married within 2 weeks, and now they've been married for more than 30 years. Rose noted that the local Baptist church refused to marry them because they were divorced (he was Baptist, she was Methodist), so they got married at a Presbyterian church. Here is their Matrix:

	George	Rose	Matrix Points:
Religion (importance: 1–4)	Christian— Presbyterian (2)	Christian— Presbyterian (2)	♥
Education	Some college	Doctorate	–
Spending (1–4)	3	3	♥
Politics (1–4)	2	3	♥
Environment:			
▪ Birth Order	Firstborn of two	Firstborn of three	♥
▪ Clean (1–4)	3	2	♥
Chemistry	Type O	Type O	♥
Togetherness	Traveling, talking, music, art, architecture, symphony, antiquing		♥
Matrix Score:			7

They have attended Presbyterian churches and have sung in the choir together ever since. ...So for the school board leader and the newspaper publisher, the second time's the charm.

Marriage After Being Widowed

Profile SM-2: Robert and Marjorie

"We have only been married 15 months but knew each other over 20 years," says Marjorie. "We were good friends first and fell in *love* [Marjorie underlined the word *love*] after both our spouses died. God has truly blessed us in finding so much happiness at our age."

What a beautiful love story! Their Ideal score of 8 reflects their shared Religion, Spending, Politics, Environment (Cleanliness), Chemistry, and Togetherness factors, plus their similar-enough Education factor, as well as their perfect matchup as a Firstborn (him) and a Virtual Firstborn (her). Her status as a Middle-Child made her compatible with him even without the 5-year age gap between herself and her next-oldest sibling, but that gap makes her even more aligned with him. Here is their Matrix:

141

	Robert	Marjorie	Matrix Points:
Religion (importance: 1–4)	Christian—Presbyterian (2)	Christian—Presbyterian (1)	♥
Education	Some college	High school	♥
Spending (1–4)	2	2	♥
Politics (1–4)	1	1	♥
Environment:			
▪ Birth Order	Firstborn of two	Thirdborn of six (5 years younger than her next-oldest sibling)	♥
▪ Clean (1–4)	2	2	♥
Chemistry	Type O	Type O	♥
Togetherness	Golf, walking, dancing, talking, traveling		♥
Matrix Score:			8

Final Thoughts on Second Marriages...

Second marriages often lack a full complement of Matrix compatibility, which is probably due to a combination of (1) the smaller percentage of available singles, simply due to folks already being married, and (2) the tendency of people to look more for stability and deep friendship, as opposed to being quite so ready to get fired up about things.

In fact, of all 255 couples responding to the Matrix survey, only one married couple were on opposite ends of the Education spectrum, and theirs was a second marriage: John and Esther. She had completed high school, and he had earned his doctorate. Both were widowed at relatively young ages, and they each had children by their first marriages...and they and their spouses had all been very close friends with each other. After their spouses died, their friendship deepened. They were happily married for almost 40 years.

If you're on your second marriage, you've already had a harsh lesson in humbleness during the divorce or death of your previous spouse, so you know you have to relent about some things. This study's second-marriage couples tended to have a serene demeanor about them when they were around each other, seemingly reflecting a gratitude toward life that the others didn't display as consistently as this group did.

Chapter 13: Why Some Marriages Don't Work Out

When I asked some of the divorced participants to expound on why their marriages didn't work out, the results were eerily similar. Only two cited infidelity; all of the others said that there were many annoying differences that just kept building up to the point of absolute frustration with each other.

1. Assuming You Can (or Should) Change the Other Person

One of the biggest mistakes people make (especially women) in romantic relationships is assuming that their partner can be changed to be more agreeable after marriage. If you find yourself thinking, "This isn't important to them now, but I'll gently influence them to see it my way"— whether the issue be related to Religion, Education, Spending, Politics, Environment (Cleanliness), or activities you do Together. This is a naïve approach no matter how right you believe you are, and it will lead down a messy road of frustration and heated arguments if the issues aren't addressed beforehand. And that might mean the end of the relationship, but that's what dating is for—let it end—don't force it or rationalize it.

Don't go into a relationship with a "sacrificial lamb" mentality about yourself, such as marrying the other person with the idea that you will eventually convert them to your Religion—and rationalizing that even if it doesn't turn out as you hoped, it will still be a worthwhile cause. None of the books of any of the major world Religions encourage this in the realm of marriage, and the reason is because it is a fruitless mission.

2. Because It's a Sign (but it isn't, really)

One couple shared the same birthday. They even waited until their birthday fell on a Saturday before they got married. But in retrospect, that long engagement lasted longer than the marriage itself, and it fell apart— having the same birthday is fun, but it doesn't mean God wants you to marry each other.

A similar sidetrack that's often misinterpreted as a sign is horoscopes. Keep the full calendar available! And yet another is names. Jamie and Jamie shouldn't get married just because they're pretty much attracted to each other and, hey, they have the same name! And it also didn't work out when two people whose last name was Taylor got married. (I dated another Collins, but alas, we didn't make it as far as the altar.)

3. "He married her for her cute little lisp, and he divorced her for her cute little lisp"

A pre-marriage church group-counseling session I attended with my husband (who was then my fiancé) began with each couple declaring to the group what they "admire most" about each other. Most of the participants said how much they love each other's sense of humor, trustworthiness, warmth, and other character issues. But several of the men said they most liked their fiancée's lips, eyes, etc.; several women cited their fiancé's hair or other physical feature.

These superficial reasons are a huge red flag. Our bodies get old and gray and wrinkly over time! If physical attributes are what you admire most about the other person, the relationship is too shallow, and you need to keep looking. Remember that you should be romantic best friends first, and that alone will keep the relationship strong even through illness and age. Physical features will fade, and fascinating habits or unusual traits will become less intriguing after a while. Those distinctions will become commonplace over time and will thus lose their luster, such as a fabulous British accent or a powerful profession.

4. "I'd better settle down now—the biological clock is ticking"

Be sure to date lots of different types of people—there's no rush! After all, many of us have preconceived ideas about the type of person we might marry. But as you meet and get to know different types, you'll find that there are certain characteristics that you consistently like. You'll learn a lot about people in the process, and you'll even learn more about *yourself*.

Later in this chapter, you'll meet one of the survey's divorced couples, Catherine and John (Profile D-2). John had a body odor that bothered her even when they were dating, but Catherine was in a hurry to get married, so she ignored it; as the years went by, it became more and more repulsive. If someone has a body odor or bad breath condition that bothers you, don't let the relationship continue as anything more than friends. Catherine isn't the only one who reported this as an issue that became more and more of a turnoff over time.

5. "No one will marry this person unless I do!"

My Dad is a minister and has counseled many couples over the years, and one of his mantras has always been: "Don't marry someone because you feel sorry for him!" The fact that this is such a mantra makes me think he's probably seen this happen fairly often, surprisingly.

If you have extreme difficulty letting people down, be very picky about whom you date. You might find yourself thinking, "I'll just go out with this person once, since no one ever wants to go out with them." But pity can be dangerous for a people-pleaser, because how and when are you going to cut the cord? It's best to nip it in the bud and not agree to a first date to begin with. Otherwise, you could get stuck in a relationship and end up wasting precious time—or worse.

6. Your Family Thinks You Should Marry This Person

Remember the tragedy of Prince Charles and Princess Diana of Wales? They were both of noble birth (which is a combined Spending/Politics/Environment factor), which was important to his family. But those few issues may be where their similarities ended. One could argue that Charles was raised in an environment where extramarital affairs were quietly part of the family culture anyway, but I would argue that he may have been able to break that trend if he had married someone more like himself to begin with. Likewise, Diana might have led a happier life if she would have dated beyond age 19 (when she married Charles) and married someone more fun-loving and warm like herself.

My point isn't to pour blame on them, but rather to point out the lesson we can learn from them. Marriage isn't about marrying each other's family. The institution of marriage means you put each other first, above everyone else on the Earth, including your parents and children. Ironically, the glue of your commitment together usually makes your (both of your) relationships with your parents and children even stronger.

The issue of family also brings us to heritage. You might be a Greek American, but that doesn't mean that if you find an attractive but only mildly compatible Greek person that it's time to take the plunge. It might feel comfortable because you have the same culture, but how about your conversations for the rest of your life? You need to have the RESPECT attributes in line with each other.

7. The Chemistry Is So Strong (...but that's all)

One problem with a marriage that's based solely on physical attraction is that you'll begin to constantly gripe with each other, because

145

you'll both feel stuck. There's not much to talk about, not much to do. Typically, this means the woman engages in constant nagging, and the man just stops talking to her about anything important—because she'll probably just find something to criticize anyway.

Another problem with having only the "C" in the RESPECT acronym is wanderlust. If you aren't satisfying each other's spiritual, intellectual, and emotional needs, you will start finding that cute or interesting coworker awfully tempting. And this isn't one-sided: Both women and men have to find someone who will listen to their thoughts and be interested in their activities and worries, and for venting at the end of a long day.

The funny song that goes, "You say po-TAH-to, I say po-TAY-to" pokes fun at unions in which a couple does nothing but bicker, and it ends in the proverbial saying, "Let's call the whole thing off." If you two disagree more often than you agree, you need to stop dating each other. (Note: This book focuses on actions to take **before** marriage; if you are already married and this describes your situation, please see a good counselor or pastor.)

The aforementioned failed marriage between Prince Charles and Diana also brings us to the issue of unrequited love, which he had with Camilla (whom he later married). High-school reunions and other events tend to bring out people from our past with whom we might have never resolved our feelings. Once you're married, the bond must be strong enough to enable you to withstand those old feelings and laugh them off.

Lessons from Divorcées

One woman recalls one of the "red flag" dates she had with the man who is now her ex-husband. They were out to dinner at a nice restaurant, having a fun time. He suddenly reached over and yanked out the hairpiece she was wearing. "He didn't like it, so he just pulled it out!" she said. She now wishes she would have ended the relationship at that point.

Each divorced couple in the survey had some things in common to begin with, thus explaining what drew them to the point of marriage. However, they consistently had strong differences in Spending and Togetherness. Several couples first filled out the survey as a married couple and then later got divorced, and most of those lacked the Chemistry factor.

A Twentysomething Divorce

Profile D-1: Steve and Jennifer

Jennifer and Steve had only been married a few years when the relationship fell apart. "[He] and I just drifted apart," recalls Jennifer. "By the time we decided to work on it, we were both so angry, we decided this [divorce] was the best option. I still love him. Sometimes I wonder if this was a mistake."

What advice would she like to pass along from what she learned?

"The small things matter the most—a hello kiss and hug or a goodnight. Because once you stop, it is gone and it is hard to get it back.

"Also, priorities. [His] job was important to him and seemed to always take precedence over me. I say 'seemed' because that was my feeling; he would not agree. Maybe I just should have spoken up more. [And] I have learned that even though my dogs are important, they cannot replace and should not take top priority over a spouse." Jennifer and Steve were one of the several A&O couples who filled out the Matrix survey about their marriage and then filed for divorce within the following year.

	Steve	Jennifer	Matrix Points:
Religion (importance: 1–4)	Christian (3)	Christian (2)	♥
Education	Some college	Bachelor's degree	♥
Spending (1–4)	3	3	♥
Politics (1–4)	1	3	–
Environment:			
▪ Birth Order	Firstborn of two	Lastborn of two (3 years younger than her older sibling)	–
▪ Clean (1–4)	2	1	♥
Chemistry	Type A	Type O	–
Togetherness			–
Matrix Score:			4

Their Matrix is telling, scoring only a 4. Jennifer and Steve are notably disparate in the areas of Politics, Environment (Birth Order), and Chemistry, and they didn't list any Togetherness activities at all. They do match well enough in Religion, Education, Spending, and Cleanliness.

A Thirtysomething Divorce

Profile D-2: John and Catherine

Catherine and John comprise another of the recently divorced couples. As a Puerto Rican who was born and raised in New York City, she pressured herself to get married young—so she was indeed engaged to John at age 21 and married at 23. She says he seemed like a good man, responsible and with integrity. In retrospect, Catherine says his engaging voice was what first attracted her to him; but this later became "the most annoying thing!" she says.

After 5 years of marriage, she felt that their communication wasn't good; about a year after that, they had the first of their two children. John's father had had an affair and maintained a negative view of his own marriage with John's mother, so a happy marital relationship was probably never modeled very well for John to emulate. Catherine notes that she always sensed that something was bothering him, but he was always so stressed over his job that he didn't feel like listening or having an in-depth talk after a long day at work. He wouldn't agree to get a babysitter for their kids so they could go out together, and this truly bothered Catherine.

They eventually saw a therapist, but it was too late to mend the tears. "I never felt like we were on the same page," says Catherine. "Years flashed by…" and she thought they would eventually grow together and develop a deeper relationship, but instead the marriage just stagnated to the point of feeling "trapped." She also relates that the whole relationship was "all about sex," but she felt emotionally neglected.

As mentioned earlier in this chapter, Catherine also recalls that John had a body odor that she didn't particularly care for, even when they were still dating—and it became more of a turnoff the longer they were together. Here is their Matrix:

	John	Catherine	Matrix Points:
Religion (importance: 1–4)	Christian—Catholic (1)	Christian—Catholic (1)	♥
Education	Bachelor's degree	Bachelor's degree	♥
Spending (1–4)	3	3	♥
Politics (1–4)	4	4	♥
Environment:			
▪ Birth Order	Firstborn of three	Lastborn of three (2 years younger than her older sibling)	–
▪ Clean (1–4)	3	1	–
Chemistry	Type O	Type O	♥
Togetherness	Movies/shows and lounging (him); going out anywhere (her)		–
Matrix Score:			5

Although John did list "movies/shows" as a Togetherness activity, they then listed opposite things as everyday activities, and that's all—and given Catherine's input regarding her need to go out and his refusal to hire a babysitter so they could, they definitely had a strain in that area. So they don't get a point for Togetherness. Their Matrix score is therefore 5, which is usually too weak to sustain a marriage.

Divorce after Infidelity

Profile D-3: Nathan and Stephanie

One divorced participant, Stephanie, ended her marriage because her husband, Nathan, had an affair; but she now wishes she wouldn't have divorced him. (You'll recall that Jennifer in Profile D-1 earlier in this chapter said the same thing about her divorce.) Notice that Stephanie and Nathan actually score a 7 on the Matrix scale even without knowing their Chemistry factor:

	Nathan	Stephanie	Matrix Points:
Religion (importance: 1–4)	Christian—Catholic (3)	Christian—Baptist (3)	♥
Education	Bachelor's degree	Some college	♥
Spending (1–4)	4	3	♥
Politics (1–4)	3	3	♥
Environment:			
▪ **Birth Order**	Second of three (2 years younger than his older sibling)	Lastborn of two (2 years younger than her older sibling)	♥
▪ **Clean (1–4)**	1	1	♥
Chemistry	(not available)	(not available)	–
Togetherness	Travel, golf, social events		♥
Matrix Score:			7

Although it's difficult to be the "bigger person"—it's much easier to rationalize that infidelity is the quintessential reason, and indeed the Biblical reason, to seek divorce (and the revenge of filing divorce papers would feel *so* good)—it's good to at least try, and get lots of counseling and start over. After all, there was a reason the two people married each other in the first place.

Once you're married, if you find yourself becoming overwhelmed with temptation to have an affair, to the point of planning time alone with the tempting person, it's time to look for a way to stop seeing that other person on such a regular basis. If you see that person at work, look for another job; if they're at your church, go church-shopping and find another church to attend instead. Also, confess your temptations and thoughts to a trusted (repeat: **trusted**) friend or relative. It's strange how confessing something tends to take all the intrigue out of a situation.

I sat horrifyingly embarrassed as I watched the movie "Fatal Attraction" at a movie theater with my parents and sister. In the movie, Michael Douglas' character has a beautiful wife and daughter, and he becomes attracted to a loose woman he meets at work (played by Glenn Close, who was made to look a bit crazy by the makeup and hair artists!) who isn't even as attractive as his wife. She seduces him by promising to be "very discreet," and they have an affair.

I incredulously remarked to my Dad after the movie, "But I thought his wife was *much* prettier than the other woman! It isn't realistic that he would have an affair with *her!*"

His response surprised me. "Yes, that's often the case. The wife is usually prettier than the woman with whom a man has an affair."

Indeed, studies show—and counselors frequently observe—that people don't usually stray from their marriage just because of physical attraction. Rather, even for men, it's usually to get a level of attention they're not getting at home. This brings us to the point that you have to keep it fresh: Visit new places together (even locally), plan weekend getaways, and do different things together. Togetherness is so, so important. And in the meantime, kiss each other every morning, every evening, before leaving for work, and after coming home from work. Guard your marriage like you'd guard your own life.

Divorce After Infatuation (A False Sense of Chemistry)

Profile D-4: Charles and Susan

Susan married her college professor. "He was 13 years older," she recalls. "It was an infatuation that wore thin." He was noticeably more religious and much more conservative than she, and the marriage's foundation was on shaky ground (infatuation) to begin with.

While Charles and Susan certainly have a number of things in common, there are some glaring dissimilarities between them in the areas of Religious importance and Politics. If two people always have to have superficial conversations and avoid hot-button topics altogether—after all,

Religion and Politics are those deep, worldview-perspective topics—then where is the depth to the relationship? Here is their Matrix:

	Charles	Susan	Matrix Points:
Religion (importance: 1–4)	Christian (1)	Christian (3)	–
Education	Doctorate	Bachelor's degree	♥
Spending (1–4)	4	3	♥
Politics (1–4)	1	3	–
Environment:			
▪ Birth Order	Lastborn of two (2 years younger than his older sibling)	Third of five (1 year younger than her next-oldest sibling)	♥
▪ Clean (1–4)	3	2	♥
Chemistry	(not available)	(not available)	–
Togetherness	Biking, skiing, eating out, traveling, watching TV		♥
Matrix Score:			5

Because Susan pointed out that Charles was "noticeably" more religious, they don't get a point for Religion—that was obviously a sticking point for her. Even if we found out that they had compatible Chemistry, that would only be a score of 6. The goal is to score 7 or 8 on the Matrix scale, and this exemplifies why every piece of the puzzle is important.

Final Thoughts on Why Some Marriages Don't Work Out...

It's always better to learn from others' mistakes rather than messing up on our own. Let's face it: The people who insist on making their own mistakes keep screwing up! That's because even when we implement the lessons that others have taught us, we still go through humbling lessons simply because we're human—so it's better to start ahead of the game rather than starting from scratch. In the meantime, as you play the dating game, pay attention to your instincts. Sometimes our subconscious mind is more perceptive than our conscious mind. And ask trusted friends or relatives (preferably optimists who can be honest with you) for their input whenever you have qualms.

When lessons do come, though, we can stand up, shake it off, and move on with newfound wisdom that we can later share with others, just as the kind folks featured in this chapter have done for us.

Chapter 14: Meeting People

When I went off to college, my Dad told me to "play the field." I was surprised at his advice—did he really want me to date a lot of different guys? Didn't that *bother* him? Aren't you supposed to learn about relationships and loyalty when dating, and practice not "flitting about"?

It sounded like a paradox, but he was right. You need to meet and get to know many different people of the opposite sex in order to narrow down what you like and what you don't like—you don't *start out* with an already narrowed search, lest you someday feel a pang of how green the grass looks on the other side of the proverbial fence. You'll already know what it's like on the other side of the fence if you don't limit your boundaries to begin with; this way, you'll be less apt to wistfully wish you'd wandered over there, because you'll already know what others are like—and you'll know that everyone is imperfect.

You may meet your future spouse on the Internet, at a political rally, at church or temple, at work, through a mutual friend, etc. Be flexible, and don't give yourself unnecessary limitations. Let God surprise you.

Meeting at Work

Some people have a "policy" not to date anyone from work, but the problem with this is that it unnecessarily excludes lots of perfectly good dating candidates. After all, if two people work in the same place, they're likely to have similar general backgrounds—and it certainly provides automatic fodder for conversation!

The reason Professional Extra Credit is awarded a Matrix point to couples who share the same general profession is because *commonality* is what you're looking for. That's not to say that your job should be the only thing, or even the most major thing, in your relationship (after all, layoffs are a fact of life, and people can change professions), but work can provide a wide array of options for dating.

However, I would caution to **beware of the foxhole effect**. When you work 8 hours a day, 5 days a week, next to someone of the opposite sex, even if the person initially was repulsive to you, it's not unusual to develop a false sense of attraction toward that person—and it's often a mutual attraction for this very reason (the foxhole effect). So go ahead and date the other person if they're single, and be sure to evaluate the person's background with yours using the Matrix scale. As long as you don't have a disparate working relationship like boss-and-secretary, go ahead and give yourselves a point for Professional Extra Credit!

One couple who met at work are Marcus and Sandra (Profile S-3 in the Spending chapter). She worked for a newspaper, and he was being interviewed for a position at the paper; his interview was in December, so they actually met at the company's Christmas party while the organization was trying to woo him to join their ranks. But Marcus didn't eat at the party, and when he realized his hotel's room service was closed for the evening, he used it as an excuse to call Sandra—and they went out for a late-night snack/dinner together.

After returning home to the U.S. Virgin Islands, Marcus says he had two weeks to decide whether or not to take the job in Florida. "I wrote to Sandra the entire time I was there considering whether to accept the job," he says. "I have no regrets…. December 15th is our wedding anniversary."

I asked him what piqued his interest in Sandra, and he said she was "quiet, gentle and reserved in the way she carried herself, physically attractive and in general someone that I sensed I would like to have as a friend." He explains that neither of them was looking for a relationship when they met. "In essence, we found each other through friendship without the expectation of developing a dating relationship. … Sandra's genuine friendship and later demonstrated loyalty restored my faith in women and long-term relationships."

Meeting via the Web

Once you've gotten to the point where you've already dated a lot of people and you feel like you might be ready to meet "the one" and settle down, it's a great idea to go surfing! Try matchmaking Web sites where you can look for certain types of people, such as relationships.com and jdate.com.

One 36-year-old Jewish woman muses how she finally found Mr. Right on jdate.com, a site where Jewish people can meet fellow Jewish folks. She'd had a long-term relationship with a man who never asked her to marry him—she kept waiting and waiting, to no avail—so she'd spent a number of perfectly good years on him. After finally breaking up with him, she tried the "speed dating" and other venues, and she also signed up on jdate.com. Bingo!

"Last week, I put the Windex in the refrigerator!" Melissa laughed. She was so happy to finally have found the right match for her.

You will learn a lot about yourself while dating, and you'll also experience some humbling, character-building lessons (such as the Windex episode!). Loyalty will come naturally, stemming from (1) your childhood attachments and (2) your own inborn personality. It won't feel brand-new. As you date different people, you will learn to weed out the characteristics you don't like—so with time, they will become more and more compatible with you, because you will be quicker to spot the red flags.

Long-Distance Relationships

Now that you've heard some really neat stories of successful dating across many miles, like that of Bert and Katia's intercontinental meeting via the Web (Profile T-3 in the Togetherness chapter), you should feel free to consider meeting people outside of your geographical region. Such meetings are happening now more than ever before, thanks to the Internet; long-distance meetings can also happen when a friend wants to play matchmaker, so you meet via the phone or via e-mail. Of course, you have to be careful when meeting random people—just like meeting someone at a bar—because there's a degree of anonymity.

Meeting through Organizations and Clubs

Go ahead and join groups, such as a church choir or young-singles group, your college's alumni club or "friends of the college" group, civic clubs like the Jaycees or Kiwanis, political organizations, professional networking groups, charities, event-volunteer organizations, and the like. Join as many as you want. Put yourself out there—don't be shy! If you don't like an organization, just leave. That's the great thing about voluntary affiliations. Just enjoy yourself and meet plenty of people, and things will fall into place naturally.

One young couple tells about how they met through the Jaycees in North Carolina—they now live happily in Alaska. Another couple tells of how their church's young-singles group resulted in six marriages among its members, including their own!

Jump In!

Now you're armed with knowledge of what you're looking for, so get excited! Here are a few things to think about as you jump-start the dating process.

Relax—Don't Pressure Yourself

That's easier said than done, right? Rehearse the adage "Good things come to those who wait." This is one of those sometimes-agonizing procedures in life in which we learn *patience!* Just enjoy yourself, and enjoy the process. If a candidate isn't marriage material for you, figure they might become a good friend, or maybe they're marriage material for a friend of yours. Getting to know people is never a waste of time.

Remember: We're All Human...With Flaws

People who complain about not being able to find the "perfect person" for themselves are inherently explaining why they can't find that person: *Nobody* is perfect! Some complainers like this say they understand (in theory) that they're not looking for a perfect person—yet once someone's faults show up, the complainer gives up and moves on in a sadly impossible mission.

If you suspect that this describes you, if you retain nothing else from this book, remember that **you're not looking for a perfect person.**

Your goal is to look for someone who's "right" for you rather than someone who's "perfect" for you. Everyone has quirks and oddities—so if you're really attracted to someone, and all (or almost all) of the RESPECT factors are compatible with you, don't be too quick to declare a given quirk as an insurmountable difference. Give it some time and see whether you can get past it, because every happy marriage involves some ignoring of each other's flaws.

That's not to say that someone's foul body odor, for example, is a bad reason to break up, though; if it bothers you now, it'll bother you even more over time. That odor won't bother someone else, so don't feel like you're their only chance at a happy life. Move on if it's insurmountable. (And be honest with yourself about how you really feel—don't ask others to make the decision for you.)

If You Have a Paranoid Side...

If you're the type of person who has difficulty trusting people because you or someone close to you has been "burned" by someone who turned out to be a complete liar and fraud, go ahead and run a background check on someone if you're finding yourself falling for them. People who are afraid of a deepening relationship, and feel incredibly vulnerable, should call or go online to places like InteliUS.com or eFindOutTheTruth.com. They can check criminal history and the like.

Don't get carried away (there's no need to run an investigation on everyone you date!), but it's a good alternative to breaking up out of possibly-unfounded fear. Save it for when you're finding yourself getting serious with someone. It's also a good idea if you have a lucrative or powerful career, to make sure the person you're dating doesn't have a hidden life. These companies can't find *all* the dirt, but they can at least help sift some of it out.

You will definitely have areas in which you differ, possibly in ways not emphasized in this book, so consider whether or not they're small, manageable—maybe even complementary—issues, or whether they might indeed drive you crazy eventually. Pay attention to your gut instincts! And at the same time, think it through. You should feel attracted and *think* attracted to the person you marry.

Focus on the Marriage, Not the Wedding

Why in the world has modern culture made the marriage ceremony such a spectacular, expensive, and frankly irreligious event? How did that happen? Well, it's time to change things around—this is where this book is worth its weight in gold for any man.

Marriage is usually between two relatively young people. That means that the parents are still financially strapped from paying for college and similar expenses, and the young couple themselves are just starting out in life and aren't (yet, anyway) making a ton of money. So let's stop putting so much pressure on this day having to be perfect—let's focus instead on making it fun and meaningful.

First of all, the wedding should be simpler than we're making it. Have it at a church. Have the reception outside, or inside the church's fellowship hall or parlor, with cake and treats and finger foods. You don't need a band, alcohol, or some majestic location. Save those things for an anniversary celebration in the future!

Secondly, consider scrapping the sleazy bachelor/bachelorette party. What if your betrothed suddenly cheated on you by doing the sort of things that often happen during these, um, sinfests? And why leadest ourselves (and our invitees) into temptation? It's a strange custom indeed: Find someone, fall madly in love, and then look at (or worse) other people naked just before you tie the knot. What is *that?* If someone really needs to have such things, then it's possible they're just not ready yet for marriage. It's better to just have a regular party with friends.

I asked a friend of mine why he isn't engaged to his live-in girlfriend. He lamented to me about how his girlfriend has such high expectations, he just frankly doesn't feel motivated to go through the ordeal. This is how he put it (ellipses are his own, not indicating omission):

"Believe me, I'd love to get her the nicest ring...but come on, we're talking $10,000+ to keep up with the rest of our peers getting married...and what does the man get? Alimony payments 5 years later when she's tired of you being broke from paying off the ring...so a guy's got to ask himself...what's the point?"

So this brings us to "third of all," which is that everyone's expectations need to be reduced. Don't let yourself get sucked into society's pressures and clever marketing campaigns, such as "Isn't She Worth Two Months' Salary?" That was a brilliant campaign by the diamond industry and put almost as much societal pressure as Head & Shoulders shampoo did for scratching your head in public! Catherine Marshall said it beautifully in her book, *Beyond Our Selves:*

"It has been said of our civilization that it deadens emotion. For millions of people in our thing-surfeited Western world, life has become tasteless. ...Strength and romance go out of love."[7]

Save the big rings for future anniversaries; don't expect an enormous one for the wedding. If you're marrying a really great person who treats you incredibly well and with whom you match beautifully, then there are rich, royal people who would trade places with you in a heartbeat. The most magnificent weddings have oftentimes led to the most horrendous divorces. Remember you're each other's best friends. Do you expect your best friend to go all-out for you, or just to be there for you?

Keep everything in perspective, and keep it realistic. Simplicity will bring the most joy (and sanity) of all.

And remember: You're only looking for *one*. So broaden your horizons to narrow your search.

Chapter 15: Cold Feet (of all kinds)

Let's say you bought this book because the wedding plans are already in motion, but you're getting cold feet. Consider your Matrix: Does your fiancé fulfill at least seven of the possible eight RESPECT factors? If not, consider those areas in which you differ. Have you discussed those issues with your fiancé? Be sure to get everything out in the open before the wedding, and don't be afraid to cancel the whole thing just because your favorite relatives already have nonrefundable plane tickets and hotel reservations—if you end up divorced, the whole thing will have been for naught anyway.

If the two of you indeed have a strongly compatible RESPECT Matrix, consider whether you're attracted to your fiancé. (Think about how you felt at the beginning of the relationship.) If you do honestly feel attracted to each other, and you're not rationalizing the relationship and not just trying to make someone (like parents) happy, the next step is to talk it over with your friends or family members who are in successful, happy marriages—they will provide helpful insights that will probably surprise you. I encourage you to avoid asking for such advice from those who have never been married, because they have only peripheral or scholastic expertise that isn't gained from firsthand experience.

Or, if you're the kind of person who makes decisions quickly, and you knew early in the relationship that this was "the" person for you, the enormity of the approaching Big Day can seem like too much. It may make you have *feelings* of second thoughts whether or not you really have them. If this describes you, grab a piece of paper and write down:
1)	Things you have in common
2)	Things you really like about them
3)	What's bothering you at the moment
…because what's really bothering you may have nothing to do with the other person, but possibly extraneous circumstances or even just the feeling that you must "perform" for everyone at the big show that is your wedding, and the pressure that everything is somehow supposed to be perfect (with imperfect people, mind you).

The whole tradition of marriage ceremonies with myriad observers isn't everyone's cup of tea, after all! Don't feel badly if you're looking forward to the whole thing being over. But don't dread it, either—enjoy your wedding. If you have some nasty relatives who will be there and you're dreading seeing them, remember to focus on your friends and the "good" relatives. They love you.

One of my relatives had only immediate family members at his wedding ceremony, but lots of people were invited to the reception. It just made him far too nervous to get married in front of a large crowd—and you know what? I was hurt that I couldn't go to the wedding. But you know what else? It was his wedding, not mine! So **have your wedding your way**, and everyone else (everyone else who loves you) will get over it, whatever it is you're doing that's different from the norm.

"What if I'm engaged to someone, but we score only a 6?"

If you think you're falling in love with someone but you two score a 6 or less on the Matrix scale, think about your mismatched areas. Are they technicalities, like Birth Order, and you don't notice the negative things mentioned in that chapter? For example, if one of you is a Firstborn and the other is a true Lastborn, think about whether you two experience any of the red flags: Does the Firstborn act like a big bully toward the Lastborn? Does the Lastborn manipulate by crying?

Is there a noticeable difference in Spending? If so, are the differences ridiculous, or are they more relative—i.e., mostly different in compared to each other's habits and tendencies, but you two actually do have very similar socioeconomic backgrounds?

Bottom line: Evaluate the areas where you two differ, and really think about whether or not they're areas of contention. Don't rationalize them away, but be realistic. If the mismatched areas are actually somewhat severe—like in Religion or Togetherness—keep in mind that if you force it, you'll both be tempted by others in the future…because we all meet other people with whom we match in 7 or more of the key RESPECT areas.

Don't Leave Your Spouse (a note for those with an ulterior motive)

Some already-married people will read this book because they're looking for reasons to divorce their spouse. Maybe you're going through a rough patch in your marriage and are wondering whether it's worth it to stay in the relationship.

If this describes you, please think about why you married the other person in the first place. As you looked through the RESPECT aspects in this book, you probably had difficulty finding too many flaws and differences between you and your spouse, didn't you? (Be honest!) As long as it wasn't an arranged marriage, you have no reason not to put some more effort into saving the relationship and keep it together.

That said, sometimes people change as they get older. If your spouse has left you for someone else, let them go and move on. If you don't go to church, find a church with nice people (emphasis on "nice people") and make friends, and they'll help you get past it. In my experience, things always work out so much better when I trust the Lord to micromanage my life. Can you say it with me? "It makes sense."

Chapter 16: A Word to the "Whys"

"Marriage remains [our] strongest anti-poverty weapon."
– Robert Rector, Sr. Research Fellow, The Heritage Foundation

Why get married? If you fall in love with and marry your best friend, you can look forward to a lifetime of fun, fulfilling times. Sure, there will be some rough patches, but most of those are just part of life and don't have anything to do (or have little to do) with whether you're married or not. The whole idea of marriage is to live selflessly with someone you really like to be with, and to build each other up—to learn and practice deep-seated respect, honesty, loyalty, patience, adoration, and love.

Though it's true that humbleness is a great lesson most people learn in their marriages, it's the kind that stems from learning how to put others' interests before your own; it's not a "humiliation" type of humbleness, based on embarrassment and resentment. A solid marriage fosters a selfless relationship between the spouses, providing a solid family structure for everyone involved.

You'll be able to tell very early in a dating relationship what your everyday conversations would "sound" like if the two of you got married— i.e., your natural banter together. Don't hesitate to bring up lots of different subjects and discuss controversial issues, because this will shed light on how the two of you handle a difference of opinion with each other. (You'll handle disagreements differently with different people, believe it or not.) Even if you have a full RESPECT Matrix match with the other person, if they can't handle issues well, you'll need to re-evaluate. Be sure to do a *lot* of talking and listening.

Finally, pray about it. If you invite the Creator to help you find success along your journey rather than trying to control it all yourself (as if you could), you won't be disappointed. You might even learn that marriage isn't for you—after all, some of history's most important and influential people, like Jesus Himself, never married or had children. (Did you feel a pang of relief after reading that? Pay attention to your gut instincts!) That said, don't close the door and spackle it shut, because it might open up later in your life than you expected.

Many scholars and theologians have speculated that the purpose of life is practice—or possibly a test—for the afterlife and developing our personal relationship with God. Therein lies the parallel to marriage. It's all about the intricate aspects of love, such as loyalty, devotion, joy, and friendship…with a core undertone of **respect.**

Chapter 8 Appendix: Blood Type Biology

Our blood type is classified by two components. First is a letter or letter combination: either O, A, B, or AB. This indicates which antibodies exist on your blood cells. Second is the Rh factor: If you're Rh+, your blood cells **do** have what's referred to as the "D antigen"; if you're Rh−, your cells **don't** have this component. An antigen is a chemical marker on the blood that can look foreign (or not) to the immune system, prompting a defensive response by the person's body if it's indeed foreign, or "not a match to myself."

The letters represent the mutations of humanity as people had to survive in various environments and eat various diets. The Rh factor represents something on the blood that was discovered that humans share with the Rhesus ("Rh") monkey.

Both aspects of your blood are of utmost importance in transfusions, organ transplants, and carrying a child. And certain trends, insofar as the letter portion, have been observed in regards to marriage compatibility in the Matrix survey and other studies (the Rh factor wasn't part of this study).

The Genetic Aspect: Your Inheritance Factors

Inheriting-wise, Type O is the recessive gene (it's the **only** recessive gene), and Types A and B are each equally dominant. As a parent, regardless of the dominant gene in your own body (if any), you have a 50%/50% chance of passing along either your dominant or recessive gene from **your** parents! You received one gene from each parent, and you can pass along either gene to a child. This is why Type O hasn't gone away from the human gene pool, because it's equally viable. You could have one parent who's Type A and the other parent who's Type B, and you could be Type O if they each had a recessive Type O gene that was passed on to you. However, if you received the Type A gene from your Type A parent and received the Type B gene from the Type B parent, then your blood type is AB, and you do not have a recessive Type O gene. (You only get two!)

The following graph shows how it works:

163

If one parent is:	And the other is:	…and you received this gene from the 1st parent:	…and you received this gene from the 2nd parent:	This is your blood type:
Type O	Type O	Type O	Type O	Type O
Type O	Type A	Type O	Type O (the 2nd parent's recessive gene)	Type O
Type O	Type A	Type O	Type A (the 2nd parent's dominant gene)	Type A
Type O	Type B	Type O	Type O (the 2nd parent's recessive gene)	Type O
Type O	Type B	Type O	Type B (the 2nd parent's dominant gene)	Type B
Type O	Type AB	Type O	Type A	Type A
Type O	Type AB	Type O	Type B	Type B
Type A	Type A	Type O (the 1st parent's recessive gene)	Type O (the 2nd parent's recessive gene)	Type O
Type A	Type A	Type O (the 1st parent's recessive gene)	Type A (either parent's dominant gene)	Type A
Type A	Type A	Type A (the 1st parent's dominant gene)	Type A (the 2nd parent's dominant gene)	Type A
Type A	Type B	Type O (the 1st parent's recessive gene)	Type O (the 2nd parent's recessive gene)	Type O
Type A	Type B	Type O (the 1st parent's recessive gene)	Type B (the 2nd parent's dominant gene)	Type B
Type A	Type B	Type A (the 1st parent's dominant gene)	Type O (the 2nd parent's recessive gene)	Type A
Type A	Type B	Type A (the 1st parent's dominant gene)	Type B (the 2nd parent's dominant gene)	Type AB
Type A	Type AB	Type O (the 1st parent's recessive gene)	Type A	Type A
Type A	Type AB	Type O (the 1st parent's recessive gene)	Type B	Type B
Type A	Type AB	Type A (the 1st parent's dominant gene)	Type A	Type A
Type A	Type AB	Type A (the 1st parent's dominant gene)	Type B	Type AB
Type B	Type B	Type O (the 1st parent's recessive gene)	Type O (the 2nd parent's recessive gene)	Type O
Type B	Type B	Type O (the 1st parent's recessive gene)	Type B (either parent's dominant gene)	Type B
Type B	Type B	Type B (the 1st parent's dominant gene)	Type B (the 2nd parent's dominant gene)	Type B
Type B	Type AB	Type O (the 1st parent's recessive gene)	Type A	Type A
Type B	Type AB	Type O (the 1st parent's recessive gene)	Type B	Type B
Type B	Type AB	Type B (the 1st parent's dominant gene)	Type A	Type AB
Type B	Type AB	Type B (the 1st parent's dominant gene)	Type B	Type B
Type AB	Type AB	Type A	Type A	Type A
Type AB	Type AB	Type A	Type B	Type AB
Type AB	Type AB	Type B	Type B	Type B

Recommended Reading and Bibliography

Some concepts in this book might have piqued your interest for further investigation! The books and resources listed below are highly recommended if you'd like to research further, and are quoted in this book as denoted by the footnote numbers.

[1] *The Answer Is in Your Bloodtype*, by Dr. Joseph Christiano and Dr. Steven M. Weissberg, Personal Nutrition USA, 1999.

[2] *All's Fair*, by Mary Matalin, James Carville, and Peter Knobler, Random House/Simon & Schuster, 1994.

[3] *Eat Right 4 Your Type*, by Dr. Peter D'Adamo and Catherine Whitney, Putnam Adult, 1996.

[4] *What's Your Type? How Blood Types Are the Keys to Unlocking Your Personality*, by Peter Constantine, Plume, 1997.

[5] www.AABB.org.

[6] Duane C. Hinders, as quoted on www.Education.com.

[7] *Beyond Our Selves*, by Catherine Marshall, Chosen Books, 2001.

Acknowledgements and Thanks

I am so proud of the cross-section of the globe who participated in this study—people from Japan, Russia, Ecuador, Scotland, the United States, and beyond; people of many colors and religions, from Islam to Hinduism to Judaism to the full spectrum of Christianity—Catholics, Baptists, Mormons, Pentecostals, and everything in between; and people of different professions and socioeconomic backgrounds, including doctors, lawyers, firefighters, police officers, 13 Protestant pastors, corporate executives, former and current editorial staff of *The Miami Herald* and the *South Florida Sun-Sentinel,* farmers, teachers, teachers' aides, multimillionaires, stay-at-home mothers and fathers, and a U.S. Congressman. Participants even include a Jewish survivor of the Holocaust and a Shi'ite Muslim survivor of a murderous rampage of Saddam Hussein's regime.

I'd like to again thank Joseph "Dr. Joe" Christiano for writing such an inspiring Foreword. I am honored that he agreed to participate in this book project. Thanks also go to my friend Laura Ogden, who encouraged me and garnered help from her sister, Janet, and Janet's husband, author Philip Yancey. And special thanks to Brad Wilcox, director of The National Marriage Project, and to Adam Levin from Credit.com, each for personally giving me a quote just for this book. What an honor.

The following participants consented to be acknowledged here on these pages; many other participants chose to remain anonymous, but I owe all of them a huge debt of gratitude for their invaluable input and feedback. (For couples in which the wife hasn't taken her husband's name, they're alphabetized by the husband's last name.)

Joseph & Mary Amrein
Robert & Patricia Ayers
Doug & Nancy Bailey
George & Mary Liz Bailey
Don & Mary Barbuto
Tom & Ann Barner
Ken & Sheryle Barrett
Ray & Mary Lou Biagiotti
Eddie & Nancy Billingsley

William & Patricia Blake
Joel & Jane Boldenow
Harold & Karen Bradley
Tom & Nicki Brawley
Cole & Helen Simpson Brembeck
Al & Carol Broughton
Paul & Jennifer Burroughs
Richard & Vickie Byrd
Roger & Kittina Renee Caldwell

166

THE COMPATIBILITY MATRIX

Lou & Marie Campi
James Chism & Laura Alonso
Tom & Connie Carrigan
Rex & Carol Ciavola
Tony & Marilyn Cipriani
David & Debbie Clayton
Kevin & Kara Cohen
Rick & Darlene Coleman
Neil & Irina Collins
Robert & Louise Collins
William & Mary Cummings
Keary Cunningham & Drew Smith
Charles & Margaret Damsel
Chip & Janice Damsel
Brian & Ann Daniels
Al & Vickie Danielson
Bob & Mary Lou Dayton
John & Erica Diaz
Mike & Meg Dickman
Wes & Susan Dickman
John & Chris Donohue
Lorraine & Chandler Dora
Bob & Joan Dowler
Michael & Nancy Duffy
Randall & Tammy Dugal
James & Nancee Egan
Chad & Daphne Elwood
Mike & Janie Emmert
Robert & Marie Errigo
Ralph & Becky Everett
Nasser & Cindy Fakhoury
Brian & Nicole Farmer
Dean & Heather Ferguson
Christopher & Elizabeth Ferrard
Bill & Nelle Flewellen
Robert & Keren Franklin
James & Nadine Fredrick
Dick & Tootsie Gates
David & Dot Geil
Jerry & Lucille Grattan
Doug & Sue Gregg
Robert & Ruth Gregory

Axel & D'Ana Guiloff
Tom & Susan Halliday
Bill & Paula Hanser
Charles & Jean Harris
L. David & Trudy Flothmeier Harris
Mike & Nora Hayden
Lanny & Allyson Heidenfelder
Sean & Nicole Heran
Steve & Ginny Holm
Patrick & Kathleen Horsch
Michael & Susan James
Jason & Nicole Jhonson
David & Flo Jones
Robert & April Jones
Bill & Sandy Kelley
David & Lucy Kelso
David & Joan Kidd
Kenneth & Dorothy Killian
Marcus & Sandra King
Adam & Karen Kramser
Michael & Cheryl Paul Ladd
John & Esther Lampe
Wesley & Yvonne Lane
Peter & Barbara Laspina
Hyrum & Barbara Lee
Larry & Ingrid Lief
Edgar & Margaret Lind
Isaac & Beth Marcadis
Doug & Carole Mazza
Ed & Louise McLean
Steve & Sandy Mead
Garry & Kim Messick
Donald & Charlotte Miller
Randall & Karen Miller
Marshall & Miriam Monsell
Mike & Sue Moody
Scott & Robin Morrison
Charles & Martha Musgrove
Walter & Janice Neely
Don & Kim Newkirk
Walt & Charlotte Newman
Jason & Charlee Nolan

Jim & Lois O'Connor
Bill & Laura Ogden
Ozzie & Susan Ona
Dan & Donna Page
Craig & Cindy Parker
James & Margaret Patterson
Jim & Doranne Peelman
Charles & Louise Peterson
Shawn & Cassie Peterson
Chris & Colleen Pinto
James & Kathleen Pippen
Jeff & Leslie Pittges
Bob & Lolly Pless
Vernon & Bobbi Poest
"Sandy" & Louise Polson
Mike & Susan Price
Ed & Mary Alice Pugh
Steve & Jodi Randall
Ivan & Heather Reed
Paul & Melissa Richards
Harvey & Rhoda Rock
Gordon & Florence Russell
Bryan & Patricia Savage
Jason & Sarah Schnabel
Brian & Tracey Schneider
Joe & Marilyn Schneider
Ted & Diane Semple
Eric & Suzi Sidman
Tim Stepien & Kirsten Siegel

Robbie & Kay Siemon
Mark & Christy Standridge
Robert & Rosemary Sullivan
Milt & Helen Swearengin
Rick & Sharon Tate
Kehinde & Kathryn Thomas
Rudolph & Virginia Thuman
Slats & Marilyn Timmerman
John & Cathy Tosner
Phil Tucciarone & Suzanne Dunn
Ronald & Sarah Turner
James & Karen Trogdon
Jeremy & Stephanie Tyree
Bert van der Zaag & Katia Rios
Karl & Gladys Van Otteren
Jerry & Joyce Viola
Douglas & Caren Voorhis
Christopher & Ruth Ward
Seymour & Roslyn Waschitz
Wil & Wilma Watson
George Webb & June Upchurch
Bob & LaVerne Wells
Charles & Bea Wenrich
Robert & Jennifer White
Ren & Tammy Wiles
Ludo & Margaret Winckel
Ken & Gail Woodcum
Julian & Kim Young
Robert & Marjorie Zimmerman

And the following couples agreed to be acknowledged by their first names only:

David & Susan
David & Virginia
Ernie & Carol
George & Diane
Harry & Mary
Howard & Helen
Keith & Helen
Ken & Jan
Kenneth & Dorothy
Martin & Mary

Melvin & Mona
Michael & Connie
Michael & Patricia
Rick & Darlene
Rod & Jill
Stuart & Priscilla
Taylor & Dannielle
Ted & Lorraine
Wes & Kelly

Many thanks to Melissa Waschitz Vanefsky, Jessica Strazulla, Yamit Sadok, Kari Mingolello, Darren Preston Lane, Amy Marie Clark, Aki Aoyama, and Christopher Cooper for their overflowing encouragement and invaluable feedback during the years-long writing process. Also, I'd like to thank statistician extraordinaire Chris Boyd. Tracey Schneider gets I-can't-thank-you-enough kudos for handing out the survey to her group of young mothers in the Durham, North Carolina, area—I was pleasantly surprised to have so many participants from that group—all these postmarked envelopes from Durham started filling my mailbox!

Input for these chapters was also garnered from Kyle Kohloff, Angela Bean, David Laurie, Leslie Lehman, Carol Phipps, Kimberly Yanchik, Sharon DiSarro, Janet Carreras, Gray Fullwood, Angie LaManque, and my sister, Heidi Collins. I also want to reciprocate the favor to authors Guanrong "Ron" Chen, James Allan Fredrick, Ronald D. Smith, and Barbara Mancuso Bouton, who all acknowledged me in *their* books. (No, thank *you!*)

My extended family is too large to name them all (I have 30 cousins and their accompanying parents as aunts and uncles!), but suffice it to say that I've learned from and have been inspired by every single one of them. My Dad, the Rev. Robert Johnston Collins, is a hero; my Mom, Ann Collins, is a saint; my sister, Heidi Lyn Collins, is an inspiration; and my husband, Ron, is the love of my life and is also the very reason I have any personal credibility in this subject at all. And my bichon frisé dog, Mustard, is my little bundle of unconditional love.

Every good writer knows that the most important part of a sentence is the last word. Therefore, that place of honor in this book goes to Jesus Christ—last, foremost, and above all.

ABOUT THE AUTHOR

Heather Collins Grattan was a contributing editor to the *HCSB Study Bible* (Holman Christian Standard Bible™, Broadman & Holman Publishers, 2010), devising its 3-year Bible-reading plan; she was also a contributing writer to *Nelson's New Christian Dictionary* (Thomas Nelson, 2001). She has published articles in Newsmax, the *South Florida Sun-Sentinel,* and *South Florida* and *South Florida Bride* magazines. She has also been the editor of independent newsletter "Thy Word Quarterly," published by the Rev. James and Kathleen Pippen.

Mrs. Grattan holds a bachelor's degree in journalism from the University of Florida. She is an ordained elder and deacon in the Presbyterian Church (U.S.A.) and is an alumna of Zeta Tau Alpha sorority. She lives in Florida with her husband, Ron, and their bichon frisé, Mustard.

Joseph "Dr. Joe" Christiano is an author, speaker, and health-and-fitness guru, and he is the founder and president of Body Redesigning (www.BodyRedesigning.com). His books include *My Body: God's Temple, Bloodtypes Bodytypes and You,* and *Never Go Back,* and he co-authored *The Answer Is in Your Bloodtype.* He is a certified naturopathic doctor who has spent over 35 years in the field of nutrition and exercise, and he is a two-time Mr. USA runner-up.

Mr. Christiano has been featured in myriad publications and television shows around the world. He and his wife, Lori, live in Florida.

Made in the USA
Monee, IL
17 July 2023

39434829R00095